# DINGHY
# SAILING

# DINGHY SAILING

## Bob Bond &
## Steve Sleight

PELHAM BOOKS

*Dinghy sailing* was conceived, edited and designed by Dorling Kindersley Limited, 9 Henrietta Street, London, WC2E 8PS

Editor    Susan Berry
Art Editor    Bob Gordon
Designer    Julia Goodman
Managing Editor    Jackie Douglas
Art Director    Roger Bristow

First published in Great Britain by
PELHAM BOOKS LTD
44 Bedford Square, London WC1B 3DU
1983

British Library Cataloguing in Publication Data

Bond, Bob
  Dinghy sailing
  1. Sailing    2. Dinghies
  I. Title    II. Sleight, Steve
  797.1′24    GV811

ISBN 0 7207 1451 6

Printed in Italy by A. Mondadori, Verona

# CONTENTS

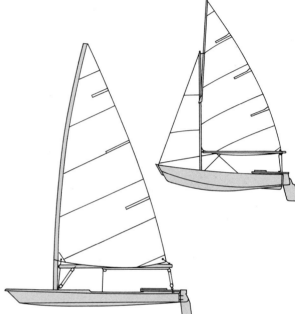

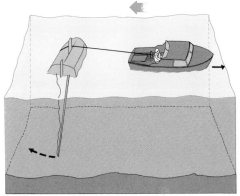

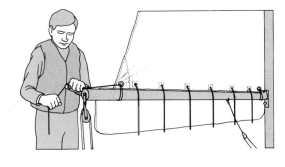

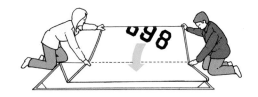

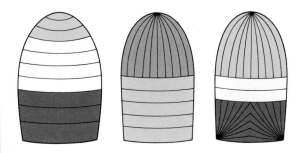

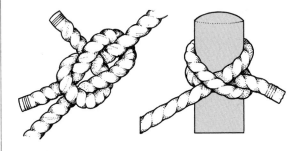

# FOREWORD

Not everyone who takes up sailing wants to become a world class competitor, but most people would like to be competent sailors, sure of their skills afloat and able to handle their boats safely and well.

In planning this book we have drawn on our considerable experience of devising national programmes at all levels of the sport, from beginners' courses to top level competitive classes. We hope that we have produced a book that will not only serve as an easy-to-understand practical guide for the novice sailor, but will also give the more experienced sailor valuable advice on how to update and improve existing techniques.

We have made abundant use of illustrations to clarify the text, and we have organized it in a simple, step-by-step format so that a novice sailor can follow the book through from the very basic skills to the rudiments of racing.

We have both been keen and committed sailors from a very early age, and hope that our great enthusiasm for the sport is passed on in this book. We also hope that it will encourage a new generation to get an equal pleasure from small boat sailing, and that their enjoyment of it will be based on a sound and seamanlike foundation.

Good sailing!

Bob Bond
Steve Sleight

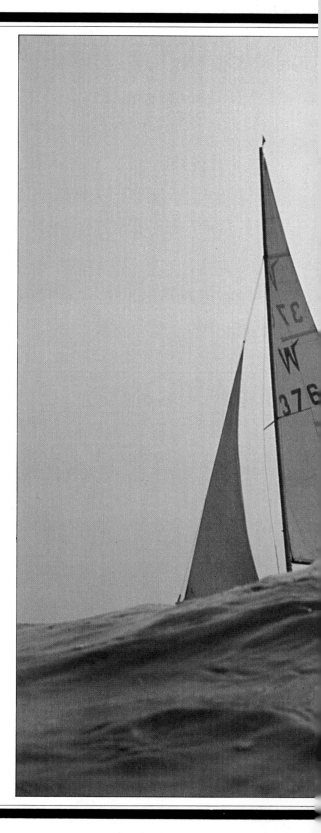

# THE DEVELOPMENT OF SAILING

Sailing is a rapidly growing sport with enthusiasts in most parts of the world. Its development as a sport, however, is relatively recent. What had formerly been the province, in the 18th and 19th centuries, of the rich alone was brought to the bulk of the population with the mass-production of fibreglass boats after the Second World War.

The sea has, of course, fascinated man for many thousands of years and from the very earliest times he found ways of turning it to his advantage. With considerable ingenuity, using whatever materials were to hand, he fashioned boats to suit his own needs and those of the local conditions. Rivers and lakes provided not only a rich source of food, but also the opportunity to move around from one place to another in a country which was often both thickly wooded and hostile. It is almost certain, therefore, that the very first boats were produced for use on inland rivers and waters rather than the open sea, since man had no knowledge of navigation, and the limitless expanse of the oceans was regarded with fear and awe.

These very early types of boat were probably simple logs which were propelled by the current. Gradually man began to lash these together to make rafts, paddled with a roughly shaped piece of wood. In areas where wood was not available, he used bundles of reeds instead, and reed boats of the same simple construction are still to be found today on the Nile and on Lake Titicaca, high up in the Andes in South America. With the advent of flints, man began to hollow out tree trunks to form dug-out canoes, powering them with wooden paddles. They are still to be found today in parts of Africa, in South America and in the Solomon Islands.

## Sail power

By the time of the Bronze Age, ships were being made of planks nailed together, and the concept of the sail had been introduced. The first sailing boats are thought to be on the lines of the model ship discovered in a tomb in Egypt in 1906. Dating from 2400 BC, and rigged with a single square-sail mounted on a short central mast, the boat was steered by a large paddle-shaped oar strapped to the stern of the boat. The Egyptians retained this form of ship for some time, and the Egyptian square-sail rig spread eastward – it is still seen today around the waters of Malaya. The lateen sail was also, presumably, an Egyptian invention. A trapezoidal sail with a short luff, it was bent to a yard arm, set obliquely to the mast. The design was revolutionary in that it enabled the boat to sail towards the wind to some extent, as well as away from it. The precursor of the fore-and-aft rig adopted by most modern cruising boats, the lateen sail is still used today by Arabian dhows. A slightly different, squarer form, known as the lugsail, was developed by the Chinese. It consisted of a single sail, made up in sections,

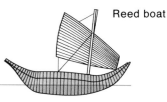

*Right, traditional rigs for working boats in different parts of the world. The lugsail, bottom right, has been adapted for use on some modern cruising boats.*

Reed boat

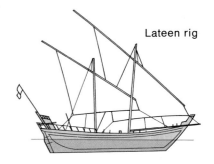

Lateen rig

Chinese lugsail

stiffened by bamboos and is also still in use, known as the junk rig. Like the lateen, it is bent to a yard, but then slung to leeward of the mast when hoisted and set, with its tack forward of the mast. The lugsail is practical in that it can be easily handled and reefed.

To understand the design of modern sailing craft, it helps to know something of the development of the original hull constructions and types of rig, as many aspects of these ancient forms have been incorporated in modern designs. Then, as now, one of the main concerns of boat builders was for speed. Early boat builders realized that the efficiency of the sail was directly proportional to its size, and the larger the sail a boat could carry the faster it would travel. However, large sails were both unwieldy and uneconomical to use, except in parts of the world where labour was cheap. Boat builders, in the Western world in particular,

resolved the problem by splitting the canvas area into several smaller sails carried on more than one mast.

This square rig, with a beamy, sturdy hull and a high freeboard, was, for many centuries in Europe, the preferred boat design for large cargo boats. As new oceans were discovered and mapped they were built in ever-increasing numbers to take advantage of the new markets.

Around the coastlines of the northern countries of Europe, however, different considerations applied, and the variety of rigs which developed to meet specific local needs were numerous. Although the square-rigged ships, well suited to sailing downwind, could exploit the steady breezes of the trade winds, the craft plying coastal waters needed a more adaptable rig. A combination of the square rig with a fore-and-aft one (a modification of the lateen sail) was developed which allowed the boats to sail

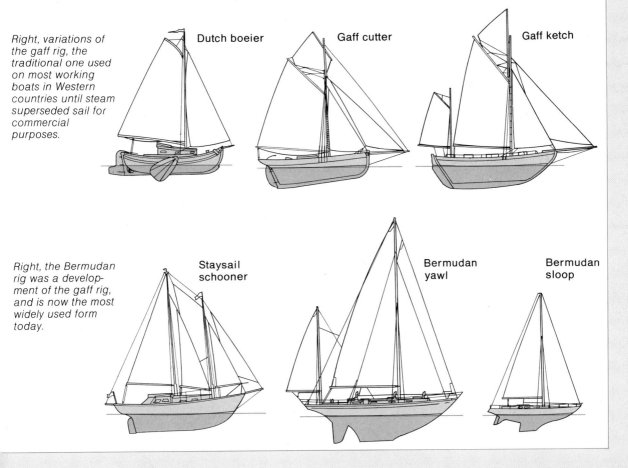

*Right, variations of the gaff rig, the traditional one used on most working boats in Western countries until steam superseded sail for commercial purposes.*

Dutch boeier    Gaff cutter    Gaff ketch

*Right, the Bermudan rig was a development of the gaff rig, and is now the most widely used form today.*

Staysail schooner    Bermudan yawl    Bermudan sloop

well to windward. Barques and barquentines, brigs and brigantines, snows, schooners and ketches all plied the coastlines of Europe, each designed for a particular purpose, to suit the type of cargo carried or the type of waters sailed in, for example.

By the 19th century, the large cargo boats had been much modified and streamlined. Competition on the trade routes to the Far East and to Australia inspired the boat designers to find improved rigs to increase speed and efficiency. One of the most revolutionary was the clipper design originating in the States, of which the *Rainbow*, built in 1845, was a prime example. "The vessel will never be built to beat her," declared the skipper. His confidence, although proved wrong some half a century later, was not surprising. The clippers could cut the sailing times of other vessels down by half. Their design was based on that of the Chesapeake working boats, with a very narrow bow, a streamlined hull and a combination of the fore-and-aft and square rig.

With the advent of the Industrial Revolution, the first experiments in powering ships with steam engines had been made. These early vessels were unreliable and much scorned by the sailing masters, but, by the turn of the century, steam had overtaken sail for many of the large cargo and passenger boats, and in the years that followed only the small fishing and working boats were still operating under canvas alone.

By the early part of the 20th century, engine power had virtually eclipsed the use of sail. However, people were beginning to turn to sailing for pleasure and recreation, and the now redundant sail-powered working boats were occasionally converted into cruising boats. Since those times the art of sailing has been kept alive by enthusiastic amateurs. Thanks to the increase in popularity of various forms of racing, boat design has been modified and improved to make boats not only safer and faster, but easier to handle. The double advantage of both adventure and a sense of freedom has spurred many thousands of people to take to small boats, and to dinghy sailing in particular.

Right, handicap racing often brings together a wide range of dinghies; here, an International Canoe, a Hornet and a Fireball are in close company at a mark.

Left, the Mirror dinghy is one of the most popular boats in the world, mainly because it has proved an ideal boat for both young and inexperienced sailors.

Left, the Cherub is a restricted class which allows the owner to experiment with hull and rig shape. It carries a large sail area for its size, and incorporates a trapeze.

### Dinghy racing

Dinghy sailing, like ocean racing, has proliferated over the last 30 years. Classes have multiplied and there is now such variety that almost anyone planning to buy a dinghy will be able to find one that fulfils his particular needs. Dinghies, though, have always existed even if the types to choose from were limited. In the 19th century, small sailing craft were to be found in every port. Like their larger counterparts, they derived their hull shapes and sail plans from work boats. Their immediate appeal was their relative cheapness and the comparative ease with which they could be handled. This remains the case today. But the dinghies of that period were very different from the modern designs. Small boats in those days, like the larger vessels, carried fixed ballast. On top of this was set an enormous spread of sail. Long bowsprits, overhanging booms and topsails were the norm. Today this outlook has been completely reversed. Sail areas have been shortened, while the ballast is provided by the crew members. Even centreboards, which were once made of heavy iron, are now made of wood or light alloys.

In the 19th century no national classes existed. Indeed, the concept of a one-design did not exist. Dinghies were most usually one-offs.

Only towards the end of the century did classes of small boats appear which could race on equal terms. The first one-design in Europe was introduced in 1887. Called Water Wags, these small dinghies were 14ft 3in and were sailed in Dublin Bay. This class, in fact, still exists today despite being nearly 100 years old.

The story of modern dinghy design begins between the two world wars. In Britain and the United States two classes of dinghy were introduced which laid the foundations for modern small craft. In the 1920s, Frank Morgan Giles, a naval architect as well as a boat builder, built 14ft dinghies, rounded in section, which were one of the best small craft of their time. In 1927 one particular 14ft dinghy was awarded international status and became known as the International 14. It was a restricted class, which means that the design and shape could be altered as long as the boat conformed to a certain limited number of measurements. As a result of this ruling, the International 14 quickly developed into a fast and sophisticated racing dinghy, owing in part to the design improvements introduced by Uffa Fox. Having had experience in the design of hydroplanes, he sought to introduce a "v" section which would allow the bow of the boat, when sailed fast off the wind, to lift out of the

*Left, Cadet dinghies racing. They make excellent training boats for young people – hence their continued popularity.*

*Right, one of the old school of dayboats: carvel-built and gunter-rigged, it was designed for sailing on inland waters, and suits the purpose admirably.*

water, thus reducing the displacement and greatly increasing the speed. In 1920, he succeeded in achieving this with his own dinghy, *Avenger*. Its impact was immediate, as it won 52 out of 57 races within the year.

The initial attraction of the International 14 was that different designs of dinghy of this size could be brought under the umbrella of one ruling. It thus opened the way for national racing. No longer was a dinghy sailor restricted to his local waters. In short, the International 14 brought about the rationalization of many designs of dinghy. At the same time, because it was a restricted class and not a one-design, it encouraged development which has resulted in the numerous classes of dinghy in existence in the world today.

In the United States, by 1931, another form of dinghy had evolved. Heavier than the International 14, with a chine hull (a hull which is not rounded but angular in section) it had a smaller sail area and was considerably slower. Nevertheless, the design, known as the Snipe, offered special charms of its own. The boats were much cheaper than others and, because of the chine hull, were ideally suited to construction by amateur boat-builders. Added to this they were particularly seaworthy owing to

their being half-decked. Not surprisingly, the class spread rapidly to Europe, and has maintained its popularity ever since.

Since the 1930s, dinghy sailing has advanced in the most spectacular fashion, but the International 14 and the Snipe still represent the two poles. On the one hand, the restricted classes offer sailors the opportunity to test new ideas in the design of individual boats. At the same time, these designs have led, inevitably, to general advancements in all dinghy design. At the other end of the scale, mass-produced dinghy classes offer sailors the chance to compete on equal terms.

The number of classes is now almost too great to be counted. They vary from small single-handed sailing dinghies, like the Topper, to large dinghies, like the Drascombe Lugger, which can be used for cruising, and sailed by a whole family. The enormous variety now allows people, even on a small budget, to indulge in almost any form of sailing they choose.

Left, former world champions Peter White and John Davis demonstrating their skills in a 505, a very fast high-performance racing boat.

Right, the unusually large sail area carried on this Bermudan one-design makes it a boat strictly for the expert sailor.

# BOAT CONSTRUCTION

For centuries the only common boat building material was wood, but there is now a wealth of different materials which can be used. Most mass-production boats are made of glass-reinforced plastics (GRP), a relatively recent innovation. In the period after the Second World War there was a changeover from natural to man-made boat-building materials, as the need for rapid construction methods became all important, in order to meet rising demand, and as the lessons learned in the development of the aircraft industry were absorbed by boat-builders. However, despite modern technological developments, there is still a large number of boats built today using traditional materials and designs as a lot of people prefer them.

The type of construction is a very important consideration if you are buying a boat, as some materials are more durable, or more easily repaired and maintained than others. However, the advice you are likely to get may well be biased, as each type has its own devotees.

## Clinker and carvel

Clinker construction is the traditional form for wooden boats, and dates back to the days of the Viking ships, if not earlier. It consists of planks of wood laid fore and aft, overlapping each other, over a framework of supporting timber ribs. Originally the planks were nailed together with wooden pegs, but later on copper rivets were used. The planks have to be thick enough to take the rivets, and, as a result, the boat is heavy. Clinker construction is not,

*Traditional clinker construction is now mainly found on older working and dayboats (below right). The cross-section, right, shows how the planks are laid. Far right and below, a new clinker-built boat in the process of construction.*

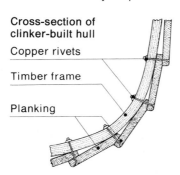

**Cross-section of clinker-built hull**

Copper rivets

Timber frame

Planking

therefore, suitable for high-performance boats. Because of the weight of the boat, and the high labour costs involved, relatively few are built today, although you will usually find a number of clinker-built boats on the second-hand market, as they are sturdy and last well.

Another traditional form of wooden construction is the carvel method. Using a similar system of supporting ribs and frames, the planks are of solid timber, laid fore and aft over the ribs, but flush with each other, rather than overlapping. The planks are bevelled off slightly at the edges to produce a V-shaped groove into which a form of flexible filler, known as caulking, (traditionally strands of cotton soaked in pitch) is forced between the joints to make them watertight. The final finish is smooth, and the boat itself is sturdy and durable, like the clinker boat, and nearly as heavy.

## Plywood construction

The development of plywood revolutionized the wooden boat-building industry, as its construction – thin strips of wood with the grains running in different directions and glued together – produces a stronger but much lighter material than solid wood. In marine plywood, a waterproof glue is used.

Plywood is very popular with amateur boatbuilders, but has the drawback that it can only be bent in one direction at a time, so that if it is bent along its length to form a curve to the hull, fore-and-aft, it cannot also be bent across its width to give a rounded side to the boat. This limitation has produced a form of construction known as chine, where the pieces of plywood are laid in sections, with two or three major angles, to form the shaped side to the hull. Single chine construction gives a rather hard,

*Carvel construction is similar to clinker and new boats are quite rare. The cross-section, right, shows the flush planks. Far right, a typical double-ended small work boat; below, a cruiser being refitted and, below right, a traditional dayboat.*

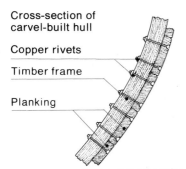

**Cross-section of carvel-built hull**

Copper rivets

Timber frame

Planking

unattractive edge to the sides of the boat, but it is simple and cheap to build. A more sophisticated form, known as double- or multi-chine, can be used, in which the pieces of ply are cut in narrower strips, to allow the side edges to have a more rounded shape.

Plywood can also be used to make a modified form of clinker construction. Planks of ply are used, their overlapping edges joined with watertight glues, to produce a simulated clinker form, and thus a rounded hull shape.

The early designs for plywood boats followed the traditional building methods, and the boats were constructed upside-down on wooden frames. The stem, transom, keel and chines were erected first, before the boat was planked up with plywood.

Nowadays, various systems of construction have been developed to allow speedy building – often with the boat being built the right way up, and worked on from the inside first. Little framing is required since the interior construction, the side benches for example, provide the stiffening for the hull.

Although plywood cannot be bent in more than one direction, another form of plywood construction – moulded wood – can. It uses veneers laid over a mould, with the grain of each layer running in a different direction to the previous one. The veneers are bonded together with resin glue, to produce a light, strong and completely watertight hull.

### Stitch and glue

With the introduction of the "stitch and glue" method of plywood construction, as used for the popular Mirror dinghy, the amateur boatbuilder can build his own dinghy very success-

*Hard-chine plywood construction (cross-section, right) is often used for small dinghies like the one below. The Fireball, far right, is a class of boat that could not have been designed prior to the introduction of plywood, which is also an ideal material for amateur boat-builders to use.*

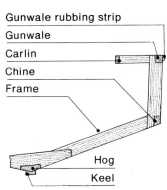

Gunwale rubbing strip
Gunwale
Carlin
Chine
Frame
Hog
Keel

fully. The plywood panels that form the bottom and sides of the hull are cut to shape in the factory and delivered as a kit to the customer, along with the decks, thwart and buoyancy tanks which are added once the basic hull has been put together. Adjacent panels are laid alongside each other, and small holes drilled along the edges to be joined. Short lengths of copper wire are then inserted through the appropriate holes and the ends are twisted together to pull the panel edges together – the "stitch" part of the construction. Once all the side and bottom panels have been wired together, the joints can be taped with resin glue to make them watertight.

## GRP construction

Nowadays, more boats are built out of GRP than any other material. It is the only method of boat building in which the material for the hull is created as the hull is actually shaped. An exact prototype of the boat to be constructed is created in traditional materials and a female mould is then cast from it, usually using the same GRP techniques that are later used for the actual boat. Since the mould takes some time to produce, and has to be perfect, the cost

of this construction is high, unless it is offset by producing a number of boats from one mould.

The mould is first prepared by waxing and polishing to get it completely smooth, and is then coated with a releasing agent which allows the finished boat to be removed easily from the mould. A gel-coat resin is brushed over the surface of the mould to form the outer surface of the hull. Layers of fibreglass are then laid inside the mould, brushed or rollered with resin as they are laid. Subsequent layers of fibreglass and resin are built up until the hull is of the required thickness. The resin sets hard, producing a hull form duplicating that of the mould. Once the material has cured, it can be lifted out of the mould, which is re-used for the next boat. Decks and interior parts can either be moulded in the same way and added to the hull, or wooden decks and fittings can be attached to the GRP hull. The material, on the whole, is easy to maintain and, being constructed in one piece, is leakproof. Although they are relatively cheap to buy, the boats can look rather like bath-tubs! However, GRP can be used to produce the rounded forms that plywood cannot.

*GRP is now the most popular building material for dinghies. In the last few years boats such as this 505 have developed GRP construction so that it can now give a lightness and stiffness previously only achievable with wood.*

# TYPES OF BOAT

There is now such a large range of dinghies on the market that a prospective buyer is likely to be bewildered by the choice. Before choosing a boat for yourself or for a member of your family, you should consider very carefully how and where it will be used. If you are likely to want to sail competitively, you should look for a class of boat which is raced locally.

The ancillary equipment for the boat, such as the sails, sheets, launching trolley and trailer, for example, are expensive, so if you are buying a second-hand boat, check to see how much equipment is included, and what condition it is in. If you are buying a boat for the first time and are not an experienced sailor, you would be wise to seek advice from your local club, and you should get an expert to inspect any boat you plan to buy.

*A Mirror dinghy – a highly versatile small boat*

# Family boats

There is a very wide range of boats in this category as they have to fulfil a variety of roles – fishing, camping, and racing, as well as providing a training boat for youngsters and an all-purpose boat for family holidays. You can often find locally built traditional boats which are ideally suited for family use. Many open boats have a fixed keel. Although well-suited to sea-sailing, they would normally have to be kept on a mooring in an estuary, river or harbour. Any boat on the lines of the Drascombe Lugger, for example, would be an excellent choice for family use. With this particular boat (and there are many similar locally built boats) the sail plan is split on two masts, making it easy to handle and giving more crew members the chance to play an active part. It is large enough to be used for day-sailing or camping, and can be used for fishing or coastal cruising, particularly with an outboard engine fitted. The Drascombe Lugger is a GRP boat, but many similar ones are of traditional wooden construction. The Wayfarer, another GRP family boat, is surprisingly adaptable. While seaworthy enough to be sailed, as it was once, from England to Norway, it performs well under sail, and can be raced. It is very stable and is, therefore, a very good training boat, although it is heavy, and would be better left on moorings than manhandled in and out of the water every time you sail.

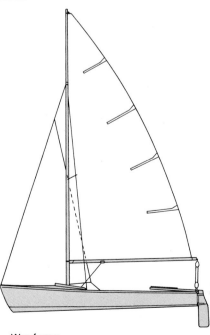

**Wayfarer**

# Racing dinghies

The majority of dinghies fall into this category but, of course, a number of boats are designed for particular levels of racing and you must take care to choose a boat which suits your level of ability, your ambitions and your agility. For novice sailors, particularly younger and lighter ones, the 420 is a good choice. A popular lightweight boat with a trapeze system, it is also designed for use with a spinnaker. There are a number of fleets of 420s, giving plenty of racing opportunities, and it is also an excellent training boat for an intermediate sailor. The 470 is a larger, more sophisticated sister of the 420, and is an Olympic class boat. It is sailed worldwide and provides good racing, being more demanding than the 420. It is an ideal boat for anyone with ambitions to go in for top-class racing. The single-handed Laser and the two-man Laser II are both excellent choices. The single-handed Laser is an excellent young person's boat, while actually providing a very high performance and demanding a lot of skill on the part of the helmsman if it is to be raced successfully. The two-man boat would be a good choice for two lightweight youngsters. Eventually, as a really experienced sailor, you might like a 505, a classic high-performance dinghy with a large sail area. It is raced worldwide, in top-class fleets, is demanding to sail, and would be a good boat with two people who are too heavy for a 470, for example.

# Dinghies for youngsters

If you are buying a boat for a young person, you should always involve them in the choice. They must like the boat and be able to manage it by themselves, if they are to enjoy their sailing. The boat, therefore, has to be small and light enough for them to launch it and recover it easily, and interesting enough to give some fun. A single-handed boat is a very good choice for a child or teenager, and will provide an excellent opportunity for them to learn a lot about sailing quite quickly. In fact, if you have two children who are both keen to sail, you should consider buying two single-handers, rather than one two-man boat: it will save arguments, will not cost much more, and will provide both children with enough competition to improve their sailing rapidly. An Optimist is a popular choice in this category, and can be home-built. The Mirror is another versatile first boat and is highly adapatable. It can be sailed both single-handed or with a two-man crew, and can be used for racing. It can be rowed or used with an outboard. Like the Optimist, it can be home-built.

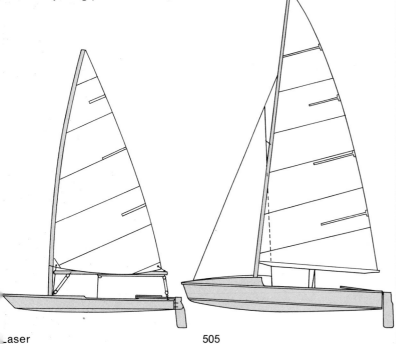

Laser    505

Optimist

# STARTING TO SAIL

One of the reasons why sailing has appealed to so many people over the years is that it fulfils a wide variety of needs – for relaxation, for sport, for adventure and excitement, and for competition. No-one should be prevented from sailing – old and young, rich and poor alike enjoy themselves in boats.

The major division in the sport lies between the boats themselves: the small open boats, known as dinghies (the subject of this book) and the large, covered-in boats with sleeping berths, known as cruisers. If you are a novice, you will probably find it easiest to learn in a dinghy, since it is small enough to respond rapidly to wind and waves, and allows you to get the feel of sailing more quickly than you would on a bigger boat.

Although this book is intended to provide you with a practical sailing course, as a beginner you will need tuition, preferably from a qualified teacher at a recognized sailing school. Since sailing can, after all, be dangerous, you must be sure that you are using safe and efficient techniques, and that you have not unwittingly picked up any bad habits. We have tried to concentrate in this book on the practical elements of sailing, and to make sure that the techniques are illustrated as clearly as possible, so that you can check your own efforts as you go along, and find out where things may be going wrong. We have covered all the basic techniques, and some of the more advanced ones, such as spinnaker handling and trapezing, which you will find necessary if you are eventually going to race a high-performance racing boat.

There is no need to own a boat in order to start sailing. In many ways, to begin with, you would be better off crewing for an experienced helmsman. Your local sailing club should be able to help. If, of course, you want to progress to helming the boat, then you need eventually to buy your own. Information on the types of boat available is given on pages 20–1. Your only major outlay as a novice, however, is on proper clothing, and footwear, and a buoyancy aid or lifejacket.

Sailing is one of those sports where you build on your experience gradually, improving with practice, and learning by the mistakes you inevitably make. Don't be put off if you find the language a little bewildering at first (there is a glossary of common sailing terms on pages 156–7) or if you have difficulty knowing where the wind is coming from; you will master these, and other things, gradually.

Even for the newcomer, however, sailing is usually good fun. It doesn't require great physical strength or stamina, only reasonable fitness, and some common sense and patience. It will teach you to be self-reliant, to be sensitive to the elements and to use your native intelligence. Many of you will find, as we have, that it becomes a way of life.

*A Mirror and a Lark, two very popular dinghies, which both provide good sailing.*

*A club race for Topper dinghies. An excellent first boat, the Topper is sailed single-handed.*

# CLOTHING AND SAFETY EQUIPMENT

The type of sailing clothing you need depends partly on the area in which you will be sailing, and to some extent on the type of boat. Most dinghy sailors now opt for a one-piece wetsuit or thermal clothing under a one-piece water-proof suit. Wherever you sail, it is always colder on the sea than it is on land, so wear plenty of insulating clothing (see below) and if possible take an extra sweater or two with you, wrapped in a plastic bag. You will need a buoyancy aid or lifejacket (see opposite) which should be worn whenever you are afloat.

*Right, a helmsman wearing a one-piece waterproof suit, with a buoyancy aid over it.*

## Oilskins and wetsuits

Oilskins are primarily to keep you dry although in fact they help conserve body heat by protecting you from the effects of wind chill. There is a wide range on the market ranging from lightweight suits, made of thin nylon, to heavy-duty PVC-coated ones, lined with nylon or neoprene to help reduce condensation. One-piece suits tend to be more waterproof, but two-piece suits are more adaptable, since you can wear the trousers or jackets on their own. In rough or cold weather, when you may capsize, you should wear a wetsuit, either with or without a waterproof suit over it. Made of neoprene, the wet suit is designed to fit very closely to the body. When you get wet, a thin layer of water is trapped between the wet suit and your skin, and is warmed by the body heat. Provided the garment is properly constructed and fits well, it prevents chill effectively.

*Doubled flaps help prevent water seeping through openings.*

*Elasticated storm cuffs stop water from running up your sleeves.*

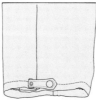

*Special clip fastenings on trousers help to keep water out.*

## Thermal insulation

Since it is important to keep warm when you are sailing, you need to make sure that you are well-insulated from the cold. If you do not wish to wear a wetsuit, an alternative is special thermal clothing under a waterproof outer garment. It is made with a thick fleecy pile on the inside, worn next to your skin, and usually comes in the form of a short- or long-sleeved vest and long johns. Another solution is to wear several layers of thin woollen clothing instead, although it is not as satisfactory since movement is more restricted. Don't make the mistake of thinking that one thick wool sweater will do the same job as two thin ones — it won't. And don't forget that you will lose a lot of heat at your extremities — so wear a hat, gloves and socks in cold weather.

# Buoyancy aids

Every sailor should wear some form of buoyancy aid whenever aboard a dinghy. There are two basic types to choose from: lifejackets and buoyancy aids. Whichever you choose should conform with the national safety requirements and should carry the appropriate approval mark of the relevant standards authority. Whether you choose a lifejacket or buoyancy aid, you must make sure that it fits correctly, and that you fasten the retaining strap or straps securely so that the garment cannot float out of position if you go overboard.

If you purchase a lifejacket you can choose between the type which has a proportion of in-built buoyancy (usually provided by slabs of closed-cell foam) and is then fully inflated by mouth, or the type which has no in-built buoyancy, and is inflated either by a quick-release gas cylinder or by mouth. The latter type is less bulky to wear. Both types are designed to turn an unconscious wearer over on his back in the water, provided of course that the jacket is inflated. A buoyancy aid gives the wearer some support in the water but not as much as a lifejacket. As it is shaped like a waistcoat, it is easy and comfortable to wear. The buoyancy aid is ideal for the sailor on inland waters who can swim, but who may capsize and would be grateful for a little extra support in the water.

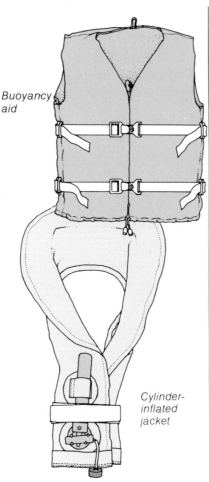

*Buoyancy aid*

*Cylinder-inflated jacket*

*The Laser helmsman, left, is wearing a standard buoyancy aid. It fits him well, and he has fastened the waist-straps securely. In this type of boat, a buoyancy aid is probably the best choice.*

# Footwear

You should buy suitable shoes or boots for sailing. Don't be tempted to sail barefoot in warm weather – your feet will slip on a wet surface and you may hurt yourself. You can buy flat-soled rubber boots, or canvas or leather deck shoes, but make sure the tread pattern gives you maximum grip. It should be deeply grooved with as many edges as possible.

# Ancillary gear

You may find your hands get sore from pulling on ropes. If you do, buy a pair of sailing gloves, with the index finger and thumb partly cut away to give a good grip. In cold weather wear a wool hat and a scarf, and in hot weather a brimmed hat and sunglasses (tied around your neck with cord so that you don't lose them if you go overboard).

Keep any other equipment you may want (sun-tan cream, lip salve, spare clothing and so on) stowed in a watertight plastic container tied securely to some point in the boat.

# PARTS OF THE BOAT

Every sailing boat, irrespective of its size, has the same basic parts: a hull, a mast, a sail, a keel (normally a lifting one, known as a centreboard) and a rudder. The hull is designed to carry the crew and to provide a rigid support for the mast and sail or sails, known as the rig. The shape of the hull plays an important part in boat performance, and ideally it should be designed to move easily through the water when sailed upright, a compromise between stability and speed. The rig of the boat can vary a great deal, the most commonly favoured being the Bermudan sloop rig, opposite. The size and shape of the sails are designed to suit different classes of boat: racing dinghies, for example, tend to carry a large sail area on a relatively lightweight hull, to produce greater boat speed. In most boats the mast is supported by wires attached to the side-decks and the foredeck, known respectively as the shrouds and the forestay, and collectively as the standing rigging. The running rigging consists of wire or rope halyards, used to raise and lower the sails, and of sheets, made from soft braided rope, which are used to alter the set or angle of the sails to the centreline of the boat. Most boats have a supporting spar at the foot of the mainsail, known as the boom, which helps the sail to keep its shape. A number of additional controls are usually included to improve the set of the sails, such as the kicking strap, for example, which is attached to the boom and to the foot of the mast and is used to prevent the boom rising.

The sails themselves, usually cut in panels which are then stitched together, can vary in size, shape, and weight, to suit each particular rig. The movement of the hull in the water is controlled by the rudder, which both helps to direct the course of the boat and to prevent the hull slipping sideways as the wind fills the sails; it is also controlled by the centreboard, which is used to counteract sideways movement of the hull and to increase stability.

# Alternative rigs

Although the most common rig these days is the Bermudan sloop, opposite, there are still a number of different types used for dinghies: most of them are traditional rigs originally designed for small working boats. One of the simplest rigs, however, is a modern one, consisting of a Bermudan mainsail without the foresail, or jib. Known as a una or cat rig, it is mostly used for single-handed boats. The balanced lugsail consists of a single four-sided sail set between a boom at its base and a spar known as a yard at its head. The sail is set with the fore part, or luff, slightly forward of the mast. A similar rig, the standing lugsail, has much the same design but the boom is fixed at its forward end to the mast. A popular alternative rig for small knockabout dinghies is the gunter rig, in which the head of the sail is attached to a yard which is then hoisted virtually parallel to the mast. A jib is normally carried as well. The rig is popular since the mast is short, and the spars can all be stowed easily in the boat. In another traditional rig, the spritsail, a four-sided sail is supported on a mast, with a spar, known as a sprit, running from the mast to the top aft corner of the sail.

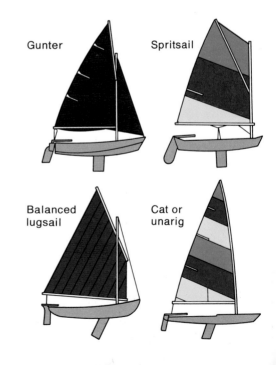

Gunter       Spritsail

Balanced lugsail       Cat or unarig

# The basic boat

The boat, right, is a typical 4.2m (14ft) dinghy with a Bermudan sloop rig. It can accommodate two people, and be handled easily by them, and requires no great skill to sail. There are many boats of this type on the market, all of which are ideally suited for the novice sailor. Some have a centre mainsheet system, right. rather than the aft mounted one illustrated on the boat, (below) In other words the mainsheet controlling the mainsail is positioned half way along the boom, rather than at its aft end. As a result, a slightly different technique is normally used when tacking and gybing the boat (see pages 52–9).

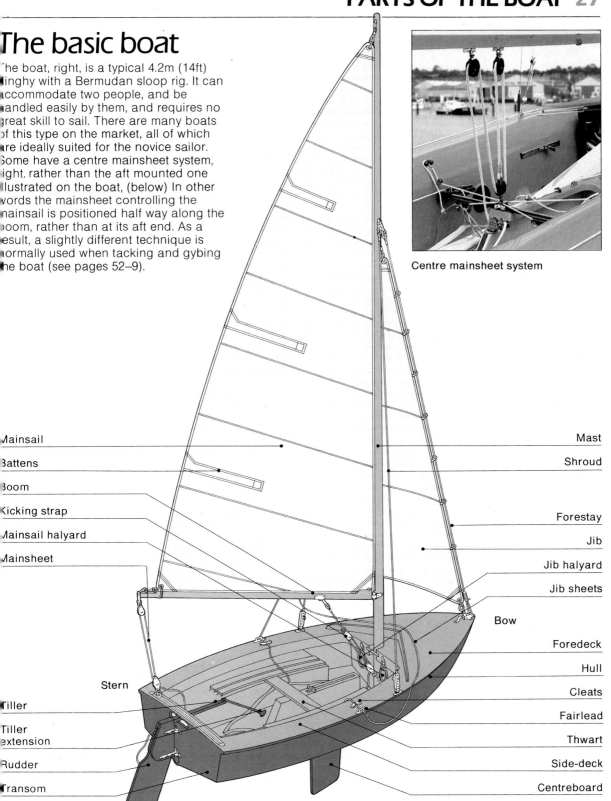

Centre mainsheet system

Mainsail

Battens

Boom

Kicking strap

Mainsail halyard

Mainsheet

Stern

Tiller

Tiller extension

Rudder

Transom

Mast

Shroud

Forestay

Jib

Jib halyard

Jib sheets

Bow

Foredeck

Hull

Cleats

Fairlead

Thwart

Side-deck

Centreboard

# Decking and seating

Most dinghies have some decking to keep spray out of the hull, but the amount of decking varies with the design. In most boats, however, there is usually a foredeck to cover in the area forward of the mast to prevent much water being shipped, but a few designs are completely open. Many boats have side-decks running from the foredeck to the transom, which in addition to keeping out water and spray provide seating for the crew. Some boats have stern-decking as well, although this feature is not a particularly common one. Almost all dinghies have a seat running across the centre of the boat from side to side, known as the thwart, which also provides lateral support for the hull. If you intend to row the boat it must have a thwart fitted. Many boats also have seats running fore and aft, just inboard of the side-decks, and known as side-benches.

# Toestraps

Toestraps, made of canvas or nylon webbing, run along the base of the boat from a point near the stern through, under the thwart, to a point on the floor of the boat near the mast. Every boat should have them, since they are essential if you are to sit out on the side-decks to balance it; they give you a secure position if you hook your feet under them. Toestraps should be strongly secured at each end, and should preferably be of the type that can be adjusted separately fore and aft of the thwart. They should be checked regularly for wear, since broken toestraps are probably one of the most common causes of a person going overboard.

*Above, nylon webbing toestraps – the ones in your boat must be equally well-secured.*

# Centreboard

Along the centreline of the hull, fore-and-aft, you will find the centreboard or daggerboard. It will be housed in a watertight casing, with a rubber seal to reduce the amount of water carried in the case. In dinghies, the centreboard is retractable and can be moved up and down by sliding the handle fore and aft in the housing. It pivots on a bolt at its forward end, and can be moved into any position from fully retracted to fully down. The controls for raising and lowering the centreboard can vary from a simple hand-grip on top of the board to a tackle system which is normally attached to the top of the board at one end, and to the floor of the boat at the other. With this type of system, the tackle is used to pull the board up and shock cord (strong elastic) used to lower it; it can be cleated in position. The main advantage of such a system is that the helmsman can operate it without having to move inboard.

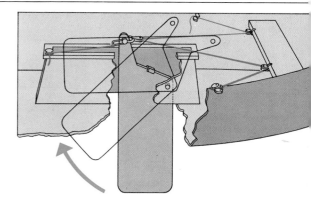

*Above, a centreboard with adjusting tackle: the board pivots on a bolt at the forward end of the case.*

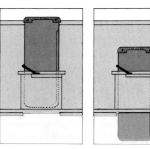

*Right, a simple daggerboard in the retracted position and, far right, in the half-down position.*

# Rudder, tiller and tiller extension

In all dinghies the rudder is removable and is fixed to the boat with hinge fittings known as pintles and gudgeons. Most rudders consist of a top part known as the stock and a lifting part, known as the blade, which is fitted into the stock with a bolt. The lifting blade enables the boat to be sailed in shallow water. The lateral movement of the rudder, used to steer the boat, is controlled by a tiller which fits into the stock, and projects forward into the boat. Most boats have an extension fitted to the tiller, attached to it by means of a universal joint which allows the helmsman to swivel the extension in any direction or plane. The tiller extension should be long enough to enable the helmsman to steer the boat when sitting out on the side-deck.

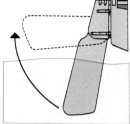

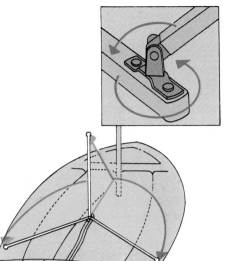

*Left, the universal fitting which attaches the tiller extension to the tiller. Below left, diagram of the planes and directions in which the tiller extension can be moved.*

*Above, the lifting blade of the rudder. A cord attachment to the blade, led up to the tiller, is pulled to lower, and released to raise the blade.*

# Buoyancy

Some form of buoyancy is essential for every sailing dinghy since without it the boat would sink or float awash if capsized. The buoyancy can take a number of forms, the type depending on the design of the boat, and the personal preference of the owner. In a number of modern boats, it takes the form of airtight tanks, built into the hull as an integral part of the structure. In others, it can be in the form of inflatable bags which are strapped under the foredeck and side-decks. The boat must always have adequate buoyancy to keep it afloat, positioned to allow the boat to float level in the water. Buoyancy bags have the advantage of being lighter than tanks, as well as allowing better control of the position of buoyancy. However, the bags can easily get damaged. Whatever form of buoyancy you use, it should be such that the boat, when capsized, floats with the centreboard just clear of the water. When upright, but full of water, the boat should be sufficiently buoyant to be sailed until the water has been bailed out.

*Right, buoyancy bags; they are normally positioned under the side-decks and foredeck.*

*Right, most modern GRP boats have integral airtight buoyancy tanks built into the boat.*

# The mast

The mast is the vertical spar used to support the sail or sails, and in most modern boats it is made of light aluminium alloy, although wood is still sometimes used. In a Bermudan rig, the mainsail is supported directly by the mast which has a groove running down the length of its aft side into which the leading edge, or luff, of the sail is fed. The mast is removable, and is positioned, or stepped, either onto the keel of the boat (known as keel-stepped) or into a mast-step on the foredeck (when it is known as being deck-stepped). The former system gives more support and control to the mast, but the latter is often used for smaller dinghies. Some boats, such as single-handed ones which carry a mainsail only, have an unstayed mast – in other words, they have no standing rigging in the shape of shrouds or forestay to support the mast. Boats which carry both mainsail and jib normally have a stayed mast.

*Right, mast and standing rigging of a typical Bermudan boat*

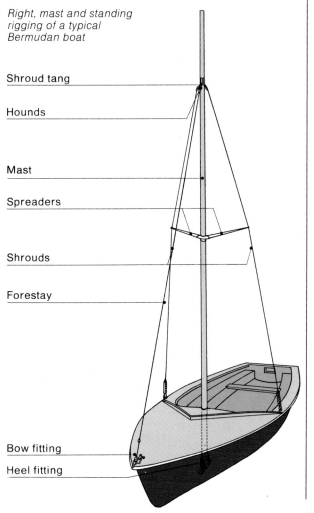

Shroud tang

Hounds

Mast

Spreaders

Shrouds

Forestay

Bow fitting

Heel fitting

# Mast fittings

In addition to the basic structure of the mast and standing rigging, there are a number of fittings which are used to attach the rigging to the mast, and the mast to the hull, and to tension the rigging. Different designs of boats have various fittings to perform the functions demanded of them, and high performance boats are likely to have a wider range of fittings than those shown below – for example, a mast ram to control the bend of the mast (see page 143). Whatever types of fitting the boat has, they should be robustly made and securely fixed. There is a considerable load on the mast and rigging when the boat is sailing, and the fittings should therefore be checked for any weakness before going afloat at the start of, and during, the sailing season.

**Mast step**
*This fitting holds the base or heel of the mast in position. It can be a simple wooden block or a metal fitting, as left, which allows some alteration in the mast position. The mast heel should fit snugly into the step.*

**Chainplates**
*These are metal plates bolted to the hull or through the sidedecks to provide a strong fixing point for the shrouds.*

**Shroud adjusters**
*Metal fittings attached between the shrouds and the chainplates to permit shroud length adjustments which, in turn, affect the degree of mast rake.*

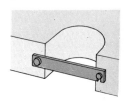

**Mast gate**
*If the mast is keel-stepped it is best to have some form of locking device at deck level to keep the mast in the gate. The one above is a simple latch device.*

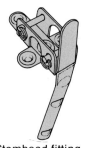

**Stemhead fitting**
*This is a metal fitting at the bow of the boat, and is used to provide a fixing point for the forestay and the jib tack. It sometimes incorporates a thin metal plate which protects the bow.*

**Rigging link**
*Metal fittings used to join the shrouds to the adjusters, or the shrouds to the mast.*

# Stepping the mast

At the beginning and end of each sailing season, or more frequently if you trail your boat regularly, you will have to step the mast into the boat. This is not particularly difficult to do alone, but you may find it easier with a helper. Modern dinghy masts, although light, are often unwieldy. Before stepping the mast, make sure that the dinghy is well clear of any overhead cables, since you will almost certainly get a fatal shock if the mast touches them. Normally you will find it easier to step the mast with the boat on its road trailer or launching trolley, with the bow down. The shrouds and forestay should be attached to the mast and tied to it to prevent them getting tangled up. Lay the mast down alongside, and parallel with, the boat and with the top of the mast at the stern end of the boat. Then sort out the rigging. If the mast is deck-stepped, attach each shroud to its relevant chainplate and make sure the forestay is untwisted, ready to be attached to the stemhead fitting. Then lift the mast into the vertical position, and, keeping it vertical, lift it into the boat and lower the heel into the step. If the bow of the boat is too high up, and if there is not enough slack on the shrouds, you may have to lean the mast aft to get the heel into the step. Once you have secured the mast in the step, allow the mast to lean forwards against the pull of the shrouds while you fasten the forestay to the bow fitting. If you are stepping a mast into a keel fitting, then lift the mast into the step without having first attached the rigging. Lock the mast gate and then attach the shrouds and the forestay.

*Stepping a keel-based mast on a Fireball.*

### Deck-stepped mast

**1** Attach each shroud to its relevant chainplate and lift the mast into the deck step.

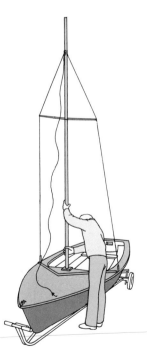

**2** Once the mast is fixed in the step, allow it to lean forwards against the shrouds while you fasten the forestay to the bow.

# The boom and its fittings

The boom is the horizontal spar attached to the aft side of the mast, and to which the foot of the mainsail is attached. It is usually of aluminium alloy or wood, and of the same material as the mast. Most booms have a groove in the upper surface, into which the foot of the mast is inserted, and there is a fitting at the forward end which is used to lock the tack of the mainsail into position. It is usually closed with a pin fastening. At the aft end of the boom there is a fitting to which a line known as the clew outhaul is lashed from the clew of the sail, to tension it along its foot. The forward end of the boom is attached to the mast with a gooseneck fitting, consisting of a metal pin, rounded at its outer end and square at its inner end, mounted on a metal plate. In some boats, the gooseneck fitting is fixed and in others it is able to slide up and down on the mast, allowing the height of the boom to be adjusted. A further fitting, the kicking strap, is attached to the underside of the boom, approximately a quarter of the way along from the forward end, and led to the aft side of the base of the mast. It is used to pull the boom down and so tension the sail, and normally incorporates some kind of purchase system to give extra power. The kicking strap, right, is a simple, basic type but most high performance boats have a more sophisticated version which allows a more powerful downward pull to be exerted. The kicking strap is removable and is usually attached to the mast with a shackle, and to the boom with a hook and plate fitting.

*Fixed gooseneck fitting which, when fitted, will not permit the boom to rotate.*

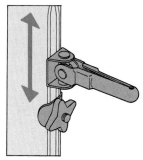

*Sliding gooseneck fitting which allows the height of the boom to be adjusted and the tension increased on the luff of the sail.*

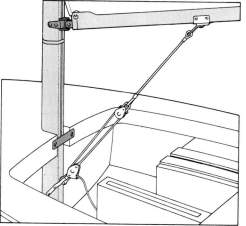

*Basic kicking strap with a two-to-one purchase system. It is shackled to the boom at the base of the mast and fits into a metal plate on the boom, above right.*

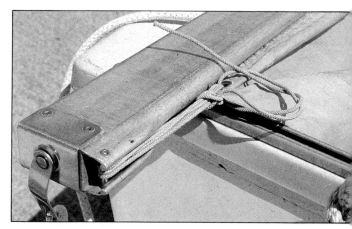

*There are various forms of clew outhaul. This one consists of a simple line which is laced through the clew of the sail and the appropriate eye in the boom.*

# The sails

The rig of the boat determines the cut of the sails – most Bermudan-rigged boats carry a mainsail and jib. Although cotton was formerly always used for sails, terylene has now taken over, as it holds its shape well and doesn't shrink or stretch, while being both light and strong. However, it does deteriorate if exposed to ultra-violet light for long periods of time, and so the sails should be stowed and bagged up after sailing. Some boats carry more than one suit of sails, using smaller sails for stronger wind conditions. In light breezes a larger jib, known as a genoa, is often rigged. Although the sails of a Bermudan-rigged boat appear triangular, the panels are cut with a very slight curve to give a fuller shape to the sail. They are normally reinforced at the head, clew and tack and have a hole, or cringle, in each corner to attach the sail to its appropriate support. The leech of the mainsail, cut with a pronounced curve, is usually reinforced with battens – thin strips of flexible plastic or wood. The luff and foot of the mainsail are generally reinforced with rope so that they can feed through the relevant grooves in the mast and boom. The jib or genoa is usually fitted with sliders or hanks along the luff, by which it is attached to the forestay. Each sail is controlled by sheets which are led from the clew of the sail to the helmsman or crew. The common parts to both sails bear the same names.

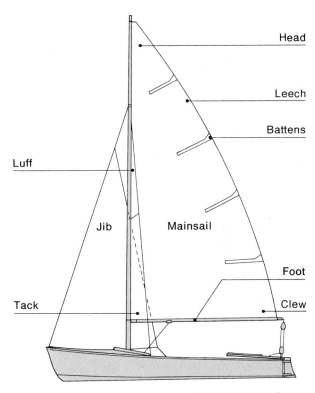

# Blocks

A block is the nautical name for a pulley and is used to alter the direction of rope.
It is also used as part of a purchase system, such as on the mainsheet, for example. It consists of two cheeks between which a sheave rotates on a pin. There are a number of types and sizes of block, designed to suit different functions on the boat. The roller bearing block, for example has been designed to operate with maximum efficiency when dealing with heavy loads.

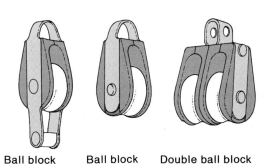

Ball block and becket    Ball block    Double ball block

# Shackles

These are U-shaped metal fittings with removable screw-pin fastening. They are obtainable in a wide variety of shapes and sizes, to fulfil different functions on the boat, and are used to attach removable items, such as the kicking strap, or the tack of the jib to the bow fitting. A snap shackle is another variation in which the hinged opening is secured by a spring-loaded plunger, rather than by the traditional screw fastening. It has the obvious advantage that the closing device can't be lost: an all too frequent occurrence with the traditional type, when rigging the boat afloat. Regardless of the type you use, you should keep spares on board the boat.

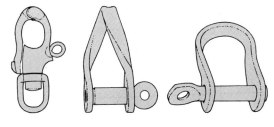

Snap shackle    Twist shackle    D shackle

# Mainsail halyard

The mainsail halyard is made of rope or wire, with a rope tail, and is shackled to the head of the mainsail to hoist and lower it. It runs to the top of the mast on the aft side, and is carried over a pulley, known as a sheave, before running down inside the mast to emerge at the base of the mast, over another sheave, usually on the starboard side of the mast on its aft face. The end of the halyard is pulled to hoist the sail, and the halyard then made fast on a cleat or, if it is of wire, by dropping a loop over a hook. The rest of the halyard is then coiled neatly and stowed on a cleat.

# Jib halyard

The jib halyard is usually made of wire with a rope tail and is shackled to the head of the jib to hoist and lower it. It runs up the front of the mast to the hounds, just below the forestay. Like the mainsail halyard, it runs over a sheave before being led down inside the mast to emerge at another sheave, adjacent to that of the main halyard, at the foot of the mast. From there it is usually led to a cleat or, on a high-performance boat, to a tensioning device (right). If a job halyard tensioner is fitted, the halyard itself should be of wire, rather than rope, which is inclined to stretch, although the latter can still be used for the tail part.

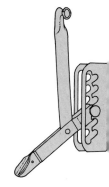

*Above, a jib halyard tensioner – normally fitted on high-performance boats to improve sail setting.*

# Mainsheet

The mainsheet controls any lateral movement of the mainsail and boom, and is normally made of soft braided rope. It is attached to the boom, either at its aft end or at the centre, and is normally left rigged throughout the sailing season. Since the force generated by the wind in the mainsail is considerable, the mainsheet generally runs through blocks which provide a purchase system in the ratio of three or four to one. An aft mainsheet is usually led directly to the helmsman from the transom and does not normally incorporate a cleat. A centre mainsheet system, however, usually has a centrally mounted jam cleat or separate cleats on either side-deck. Most centre mainsheet systems also have control lines leading from a track and traveller on which the base of the mainsheet is mounted, allowing the helmsman to set the main-sheet in any position across the boat, thus giving better control of the sail (see page 144). In older boats, or smaller ones such as some of the single-handed una rigs, the system is an aft mounted one, and in the simplest boats, the mainsheet may be led through a fairlead on the transom, without any purchase systems.

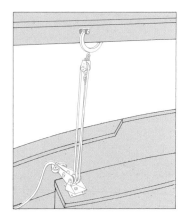

*Above, an aft mainsheet system mounted on a transom track.*

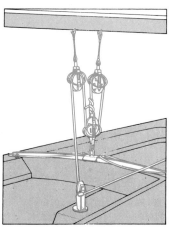

*Above left and left, centre mainsheet systems. The type, left, has an athwartships track on which the base of the system is mounted.*

# Jib sheets

The jib is controlled by two sheets, generally of soft, braided rope similar to that used for the mainsheet. The sheets are attached to the clew of the jib through a cringle, either using a shackle or by knotting the sheet to it with a bowline. The latter is the more satisfactory method, since a shackle on a flapping sail might cause an injury. Some people prefer to use a single length of rope, fastened at its centre to the clew. Each sheet is led aft from the clew, outside the shrouds, and through a fairlead on each side-deck. These can either be simple fixed fittings or they can consist of an adjustable fairlead and cleat arrangement, mounted on a metal track. In either case the cleat is normally fitted with, or adjacent to, the fairlead.

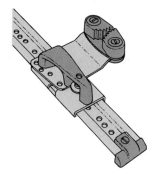

*Above, an adjustable jib fairlead track with a cam cleat attachment*

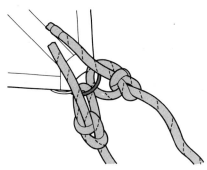

*The jib sheets are usually fastened with bowlines, as here, or with a shackle.*

# Cleats

Cleats come in a wide variety of shapes and sizes but they all provide the same basic function – to fasten a rope securely while allowing it to be released quickly and easily. The traditional form of cleat is the horn cleat (below right) which consists of two wooden, plastic or metal horns around which the rope can be secured by fastening it in figures of eight. The halyards of many simple boats are fastened on horn cleats fitted to the mast. Cleats for jib- and mainsheets are usually of the jamming and quick-release type (below left), either of metal or nylon, with two spring-loaded cams which grip the rope when it is led through the cleat, and from which it is released with a single upward jerk. Another type of cleat, commonly used for the same purpose, is the clam cleat (below centre) which is made of aluminium or nylon, with grooved inner faces which grip the rope firmly when it is dropped between them, and from which it can be released, as with the cam cleat, by a sharp upward tug. Cleats can be bought separately or with an integral fairlead.

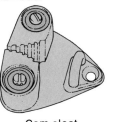

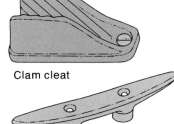

**Clam cleat**

**Cam cleat**

**Horn cleat**

# Ancillary equipment

In addition to the gear which is rigged onto the boat, you will also need some ancillary equipment. For example, you should carry a lightweight anchor and anchor rope (see page 89), a paddle or oars, as appropriate for your boat, a plastic bailer or bucket, a length of line used for tying up the boat (known as a painter), spare bungs for the drain holes in the transom and in the buoyancy tanks, (if the boat has them), spare shackles, and a pocket knife that preferably incorporates a shackle spanner. You should stow any loose equipment neatly out of the way, under the foredeck or side-decks, for example, and you should fasten it to the boat to prevent it floating off if the boat capsizes. If you are coastal sailing, you should carry some additional equipment (see pages 100–101).

# Bailing equipment

In addition to a hand-bailer or bucket, you should have some form of automatic bailing equipment, if possible. Normally this takes the form of hinged transom flaps or a self-bailer in the hull. They will only operate when the boat is moving through the water, hence the need for a hand-bailer as well. For instructions on bailing, see page 67.

# HOW A BOAT SAILS

You do not need to understand the theory of how a boat sails to be able to sail a boat, but you will find it helps to have an approximate idea of what the forces are which affect its performance. Beginners generally find it a waste of time to concentrate too heavily on trying to grasp the physics of sailing. They are better employed sailing intuitively, finding out what the boat can and cannot do by trial and error. In fact, you have only to watch young children successfully sailing small dinghies to appreciate how unnecessary a grasp of theory is, and how important it is to be able to play with the boat, sailing by feel alone. As you become more experienced, and wish to get the boat to sail faster, an understanding of the theory becomes more necessary – certainly when it comes to making adjustments to the rig of your boat, although some people still do even this largely by practice and experience.

The following is a brief description of the various forces affecting the way in which the boat performs.

# How the sails work

The sails provide the driving force for the boat by converting the wind's energy into a force which is transferred to the hull via the mast. When a boat is sailing away from the wind, the sails drive the boat by providing simple resistance to the wind, in much the same way that an umbrella does on a windy day. However, on all other courses, the sails work by deflecting the wind from its original path. When the wind meets the front edge of the sail, it splits into two streams which flow over both sides of the sail. Owing to the physical properties of air, and the deliberately designed curve in the sail, the stream on the windward, concave side of the sail exerts a "push" on the sail, while the stream flowing over the leeward side exerts a "pull" (providing of course that the helmsman has trimmed the sail at the correct angle to the wind). For the sail to work efficiently as a deflector, both push and pull effects must operate. Together they produce a driving force which is always at approximate right angles to the boom. The sail is always at more or less the same angle to the wind, although the boat, of course, turns towards or away from it on different points of sailing. The force on the sail, in fact, has two quite separate effects on the boat – one driving it forwards and the other pushing it sideways. The closer the boat sails to the wind, the greater the amount of sideways or heeling force. Obviously, for the boat to go forward, the forward driving effect must be retained, while the

sideways effect is eliminated as much as possible. This is done by the use of a centreboard, and, to some extent, a rudder, which both help prevent side slip in the water. The wind, meeting resistance provided by the underwater elements, tends to heel the boat to leeward, a factor which has to be counterbalanced by moving crew weight to windward. As soon as you sail directly downwind, the sail ceases to act as a deflector and acts simply as a resistor; the pull movement is lost and the sail ceases to work as efficiently. The theory of how a sail works is the same for two sails as for one, but the inclusion of a jib or foresail in the rig increases its efficiency out of proportion to the size of the additional sail. This is because the position of the jib, when correctly set, allows it to deflect more wind onto the leeward, convex side of the mainsail, increasing the amount of pull and thereby also improving the performance.

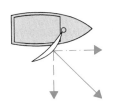

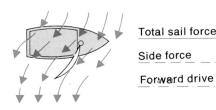

Total sail force

Side force

Forward drive

*The sail splits the airstream when properly trimmed, and push is produced on the windward side while pull is produced on the leeward side.*

*The angle of the sail to the wind is roughly constant regardless of the course the boat sails; the sideways force lessens as the boat turns offwind.*

# How the centreboard works

The pressure of the wind on the sails pushes the boat sideways, so a boat's hull shape has to be designed to allow the maximum forward movement while reducing side slip as much as possible. In older craft, a full-length keel was used to counteract such sideways movement, but dinghies do not usually have a fixed keel and use instead a retractable centreboard or daggerboard. Because the centreboard is thin, it provides little resistant surface to any forward movement, but, being wide and deep, it does provide a great deal more resistance to any sideways movement, although it cannot stop this sideways movement completely. That which does occur is known as leeway and is always present to some extent except when the boat is sailing directly before the wind.

The centreboard can be adjusted to counteract the degree of sideways force. Since the sideways force, if it meets resistance, is turned into heeling force, the depth of centreboard will affect the amount of heel, and the appropriate response from the crew. On upwind courses, when the sideways force is greatest, if the centreboard is retracted fully the boat will slip sideways through the water as fast, if not faster, than it moves forwards, but will heel very little. Once you lower the centreboard, the sideways movement virtually stops and the boat heels more. The crew then have to move their weight further outboard to balance the boat and keep it sailing upright.

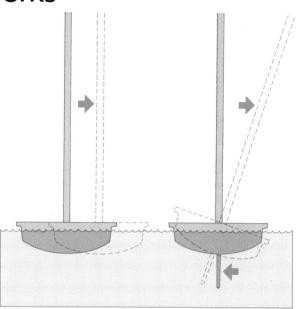

The boat, with the centreboard up, offers little resistance to the wind, and the amount of side slip is considerable.

The boat, with the centreboard down, offers much resistance to the wind, and so the sideways force is turned into heeling force.

# How the rudder works

The rudder has two principal functions – to help resist sideways force, as the centreboard does, which prevents leeway, and to steer the boat. In modern dinghies, the ability of the rudder to prevent side slip is considerable since the rudder blade usually represents quite a large proportion of the underwater area of the boat. Its most important function, however, is to steer the boat. It is operated by a tiller attachment which, when pushed to one side, moves the rudder blade in the opposite direction. As soon as the rudder moves off from the centreline of the boat, it alters the course of the water flowing past, which then pushes the stern of the boat in the opposite direction to which the rudder was moved. It is the stern of the boat that you are steering, in fact, not the bow, and the boat pivots about a point just forwards of the middle – thus the stern moves through a greater arc than the bow.

Remember that the rudder cannot be used to steer the boat unless water is flowing past it – so the boat must be moving, either forwards or backwards. If the boat is moving backwards, the rudder will work in the opposite way to that if the boat were moving forwards. Since the rudder offers an increasing amount of resistance to forward movement the further it is turned, it will act as a brake, so all unnecessary movement of the tiller should be avoided if the boat is to sail well.

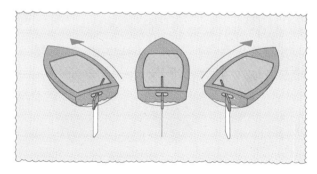

With the rudder pushed to port (left), the stern moves to starboard (right), and, with the rudder to starboard, the stern moves to port.

# POINTS OF SAILING

Since a sailing boat depends on the wind for its source of power, the first lesson for the novice sailor is to determine wind direction at all times, because without such knowledge, his ability to control his boat is likely to be very limited! Since the wind is both invisible and, occasionally, unpredictable, and as the boat will have to change course relative to the wind from time to time, the novice sailor can get very confused. More experienced sailors use a number of natural indicators to help orientate themselves to the wind (some are shown opposite) but the beginner may find it easier if a permanent wind indicator is attached to the boat, such as a small flag, known as a burgee, which is hoisted to the top of the mast or if tell-tales, strips of wool or ribbon, are fastened to the shrouds.

Having once begun to determine wind direction, the next step for the novice is to learn how to steer the boat and operate the various controls. The boat can sail in almost any direction, except directly into the wind, although the controls will have to be adjusted for the course the boat takes, either towards the wind (to windward), across the wind (offwind) or directly away from the wind (downwind). The courses the boat can sail are known collectively as the points of sailing, and the way you control your boat on each of them is determined partly by the desired course, and partly by the strength of the wind. However, beginners will not normally go out in anything stronger than light to moderate winds and the control positions, right, relate to these conditions.

Your early lessons afloat will normally be spent learning how to sail the boat on a particular course, how to alter course towards or away from the wind and how to sail to an objective directly upwind. As you gain experience and confidence, you will be able to refine your techniques and improve the boat's performance, until you reach the point where, if you so wish, you can sail a faster and more exciting boat, such as a modern high-performance racing dinghy, or you can begin to race against other boats.

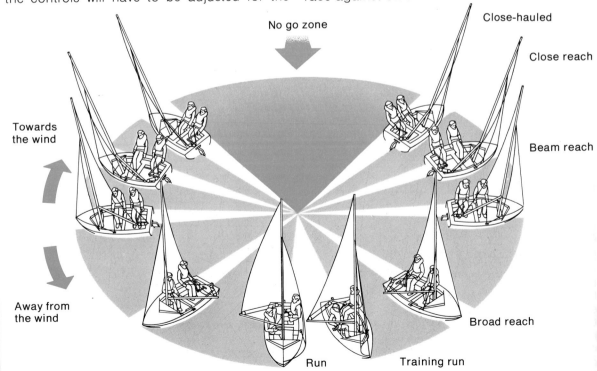

No go zone

Close-hauled

Close reach

Towards the wind

Beam reach

Away from the wind

Broad reach

Run

Training run

# No go zone

There is one sector, stretching from about 45° either side of the direction from which the wind is blowing, into which you cannot sail directly. If you try, the boat will simply stall, and you will find that it then starts to blow backwards and sideways away from the wind. The indication that you have reached the edge of this zone, known as the no go zone, is that with the sails sheeted in tight, the luff of the jib starts to flutter and the boat loses speed. At that point, you must turn away from the wind by pulling the tiller towards you, and allowing the sails to fill so that the boat can proceed on a close-hauled course.

# Close-hauled

This course is the closest you can get to the wind without the boat stalling. The sails are sheeted in tight, almost down the centreline of the boat. The force pushing the boat sideways is very strong on this point of sailing so the centreboard has to be fully down to counteract it. The crew will normally have to sit out to keep the boat upright.

# Broad reach

By bearing away even more, so that the bow of the boat is pointing away from the wind, you lessen the side force and can, therefore, raise the centreboard to the quarter-down position. The crew may have to sit in the centre of the boat to keep it balanced, and the sails can be let out until the boom is just off the shrouds.

# Close reach

If you turn slightly offwind from a close-hauled course, known as bearing away, you will be on a close reach. The forward force on the sails increases and they should be let out a little, and, as the sideways force is less, you can raise the centreboard to about the three-quarters-down position. The heeling force lessens and the crew will find they don't have to sit out so far to balance the boat.

# Training run

By bearing away even more, the boat can be put on what is known as a training run. The mainsail is let right out, with the boom just clear of the shrouds. The jib will probably fail to fill with wind, but should be kept on the same side of the boat as the mainsail. There is no side force and the centreboard can come almost all the way up, although it helps stop the boat rolling if it is left a little way down.

# Beam reach

By bearing away further until the boat is sailing more or less at right angles to the wind, you will lessen the sideways force. The sails can be let out half-way and the centreboard raised to half-down. The heeling force will have diminished further and the crew can move inboard to balance the boat.

# Run

By bearing away even further the boat can be made to sail directly downwind. The jib will want to blow across to the opposite side to the mainsail and can be set on that side of the boat, known as running goose-winged. Otherwise the positions are the same as for a training run.

# Wind indicators

Although an experienced sailor can tell the direction of the wind from the feel on his face and neck, the inexperienced one will find it difficult to gauge. It helps if you watch how other objects behave, as they will often indicate the wind direction. Waves usually run at 90° to the wind and are probably the best indicator of all. Flags, and smoke from chimneys, blow directly away from the wind. Boats moored in non-tidal waters lie with their bows pointing into the wind. Alternatively you can create your own indicators by flying a small flag, known as a burgee, from the masthead of your boat, or by tying strips of ribbon to each shroud, at eye level.

Natural wind indicators

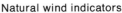

Smoke    Flag

Waves

Artificial wind indicators

Burgee

Tell-tales on shrouds

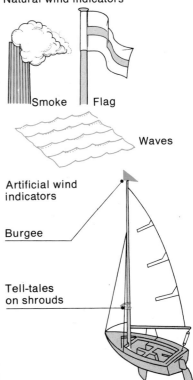

# BOAT CONTROLS

Before you can sail a dinghy you need to understand the functions of the various controls, and their effect on the boat. Although the controls may differ slightly in size and shape from boat to boat, according to the design, they all operate in the same way, and the helmsman and crew need to know how to use them to get the boat to perform to their requirements. All the controls must be operated smoothly to get the best performance out of the boat.

*Right, when you wish to alter course, the sails, the centreboard, your weight and the tiller position all require adjustment.*

## Using the sails

Apart from the driving force they exert, the sails can also produce a strong turning force on the hull. Dinghies pivot around the centreboard, and any sail set forwards of this point will tend to turn the bow of the boat away from the wind. Conversely, any sail set aft of that point will tend to turn the stern away from the wind. When the sails are correctly set there should be no tendency for the boat to turn if the tiller is released – what is known as having a balanced helm.

If the sails are not properly balanced strong turning forces can be set up. For example if you pull in the mainsail alone, or you sheet it in more tightly than the jib, the boat will try and turn towards the wind, and will do so unless an opposite force is produced by the rudder. If the jib is pulled in, and the mainsail is not, the opposite effect is created: the bow will blow downwind and the boat will turn away from the wind.

*The effect of using the mainsail only can be seen by turning into the basic hove-to position with the tiller centred. Leave the jib slack, but pull in the mainsail. The boat moves forward and turns towards the wind. The effect of using the jib alone can be seen by putting the boat into the basic hove-to position with the tiller centred. Leave the mainsail slack, but pull in the jib. The boat moves forwards and turns away from the wind.*

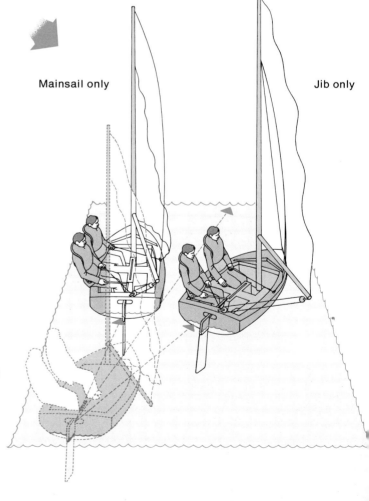

Mainsail only

Jib only

# Using the rudder

The rudder is the most obvious turning control since it was designed for that purpose. Although it is the main turning control, it must be used as little as possible, as if used violently, it exerts a braking effect. Remember that it can only be used to effect when the boat is moving – its function depends on the water flowing past it. The rudder is operated by the use of the tiller attachment, with an extension fitted if required. To turn the boat towards the wind the tiller is pushed away; to turn it away from the wind, the tiller is pulled towards the helmsman. The rudder should always be used in conjunction with other controls to turn the boat, never on its own. When sailing backwards, the tiller should be pushed in the direction that you wish the bow to move; the opposite effect to that produced when moving forward.

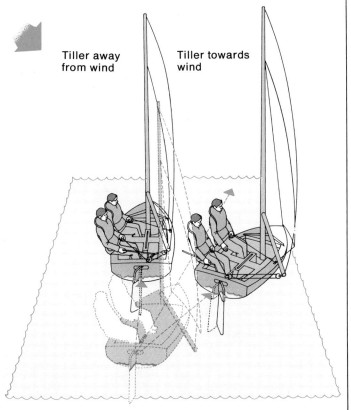

Tiller away from wind

Tiller towards wind

*With the tiller pushed away from you and from the wind, the bow of the boat moves towards the wind, the sails flap if not adjusted and the boat stops if it turns right into the wind. If the tiller is pulled towards you and the wind, the bow of the boat moves away from the wind causing the boat to gain speed. The sails must be let out to keep them set correctly.*

# Using the centreboard

The centreboard provides the major source of resistance to sideways movement, and is also the point around which the boat pivots. When on any point of sailing, with the sails trimmed correctly, the centreboard should be adjusted to remove any slight tendency of the boat to turn. If you find that you have to keep pulling the tiller towards you to keep the boat on course, the fault can be corrected by raising the centreboard a little. If you keep having to push the tiller away, the centreboard should be lowered slightly instead.

# Hull position

When the boat is trimmed correctly (level fore-and-aft) and when it is balanced correctly in an upright position, there should be no tendency for the boat to turn provided all the other controls are correctly set. However, if the trim or balance is wrong, it will do so. If the helmsman and crew sit too far forward, the bow will be immersed and the stern raised, and the boat will try to turn towards the wind, as the stern blows downwind. Conversely, if the crew sits too far back, the boat will turn away. When heeled, the boat will try to turn in the opposite direction to that in which it is heeled. Allowing a boat to heel is a common beginner's error: although it may seem as though the boat is sailing faster, it is, in fact, going slower.

*Boat trimmed with weight too far forward*

*Boat trimmed with weight too far aft*

# RIGGING THE BOAT

In most circumstances you will need a trolley for moving the boat and for launching it into the water. Some people with small boats manage without, either carrying the boat to the water, or rolling it on large plastic rollers. If you are going to move the boat on a trolley over very soft sand, you should fit extra large wheels to the trolley so that they won't dig in. Before you can rig the boat for sailing, you will have to remove the covers and put all the equipment into the boat, and then, when you have moved the boat to the water, you can bend on the sails and hoist the burgee. Always check that all the gear is in working order, and that the buoyancy is adequate. Don't forget to insert the bungs in the drain holes before going afloat.

*A fleet of dinghies being rigged on shore in light conditions before a race*

# Moving the boat

It is up to you whether you bend on the sails in the boat park or on the slipway, but in crowded club conditions the former plan may cause less inconvenience. Normally, if your boat has been stowed on its trolley in the boat park, it will have to be repositioned on the trolley before it can be moved. One person should grasp the underside of the boat at the bow and lift, while the other pushes the trolley more firmly under the boat. The stern should be supported on a rubber tyre or similar padding during the manoeuvre. The person lifting should try to keep his back straight and his head up to avoid injuring himself. Once the boat is properly positioned – if it is, you should be able to lift the handle without strain – tie the painter to the trolley handle to prevent the boat jolting off the trolley if you hit an obstacle while moving the boat. To transfer the boat from the ground to the trolley, use the same method, but you may need some help. You should take care not to damage the boat when moving it. With the boat securely tied to the trolley, pull it along using the trolley handle, rather than the boat itself, with some help, if necessary. Avoid any potholes or bumps, and, if you have to negotiate a raised kerb, take the trolley over it one wheel at a time, lifting each axle if necessary. If the boat has to travel down a ramp, take it down stern first. Should you have to move a boat without a trolley, you will find it easiest using large rollers, which can be inserted from the bow end, under the boat, so that it can be rolled over them. They can then be reinserted at the bow as they come free at the stern.

*The boat being positioned properly on the trolley prior to it being moved*

*The crew using the trolley handle, to which the boat's painter has been tied, to pull the boat along*

# Bending on the mainsail

Take the mainsail out of the bag and lay it on the boat. Find the clew and the tack, and insert the clew into the gooseneck end of the groove on top of the boom. One person should feed the sail in and the other should pull it along to the aft end of the boom. When the tack reaches the pin fitting, the pin should be secured through the eye in the sail and through the appropriate hole in the boom. Then the clew should be pulled out and fastened at the aft end of the boom using the clew outhaul. Insert the battens into the appropriate pockets (you should mark them if in any doubt as to which battens fit which pockets) and then loosely bundle up the sail and leave it in the boat with the boom on top to prevent it blowing away. Check that the mainsheet is led correctly through the blocks.

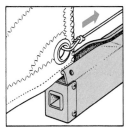

**1** Insert the foot of the sail into the groove in the boom.

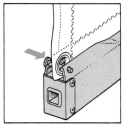

**2** Close the locking pin in the tack of the sail.

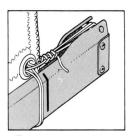

**3** Fasten the clew outhaul to secure the clew of the sail.

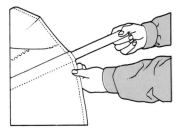

**4** The battens are inserted into the appropriate pockets. Some battens are tied in – it depends on the design.

**5** Once the mainsail is attached to the boom, put the boom on top of it, to prevent it blowing away.

# Bending on the jib

Take the jib out of the bag and lay it on the foredeck. Find the tack and attach it to the stemhead fitting with a shackle. Then attach the hanks on the luff of the sail to the forestay, starting with the bottom hank and working up. Find the clew of the sail, and check that the foot isn't twisted. Then attach the jib sheets to the clew and lead them through the fairleads, tying a figure-of-eight knot in the end (see page 146). Shackle the jib halyard to the head of the sail and bundle the sail up on the foredeck, tying one of the ends of the jib sheet around it to prevent the head of the sail blowing up the forestay. Pull on the halyard to take any slack out of it, and then cleat it.

**1** Shackle the tack of the jib to the bow fitting.

**2** Fasten the jib hanks to the forestay.

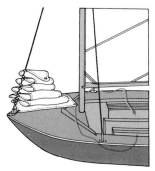

**3** Fasten the sheets to the sail and lead them through the fairleads.

**4** When ready to launch, the halyards are fastened to the head of the jib and mainsail.

# GOING AFLOAT

The first time you go afloat you should be accompanied by a qualified instructor or an experienced sailor. If this is impossible, you must at least start your sailing on a quiet stretch of water, and in very gentle weather – nothing more than a Force 1 to 3 (1 to 10 knots).

Before going afloat the boat should have been rigged, either in the dinghy park or at the water's edge. The sails should be bent on but not hoisted, and you should check that all the equipment is in working order, and that the buoyancy serves the purpose for which it was designed. If you are using a burgee, it should be hoisted by running it up on a flag halyard.

Warm and waterproof clothing, and personal buoyancy, should be worn, and anything you may need on the trip should be stowed in the boat. You should have listened to the weather forecast before setting out and should not hesitate to postpone your trip if the weather is not favourable (see also page 97).

For the first few trips afloat you will find it best to row or paddle away from the shore, as the boat can then be kept under control in confined surroundings, and you will not impede the progress of other people trying to launch their boats from a crowded slipway. As you gain more experience, you can hoist your sails before going afloat, and learn to sail off directly from the shore or pontoon (see pages 78–87).

Once you have the boat rigged and ready to launch, check that the sails are properly bent on by hoisting them on shore first. Turn the boat head-to-wind before you do, so that they don't fill with wind and, if correctly rigged, lower and stow them. Make sure you have included the paddles and oars, and insert the bungs in the drain holes before launching the boat. After you have launched it (see opposite), the crew should put the trolley away. One of you then gets aboard while the other holds the boat head-to-wind in the water. The one on board prepares the oars and crutches, or the paddles, and ships the rudder and tiller if they are going to be used immediately (see overleaf). The other person then get aboard, giving the boat a slight push, and the boat is then rowed

or paddled away from the shore. You will need to get a reasonable distance out if there is an onshore wind blowing or you may drift back onshore again before you are ready to sail off. If possible, find a mooring buoy to which you can tie the boat while you hoist the sails. Make sure that there are no obstructions in the vicinity and once you have hoisted the sails, stow the paddles and oars so that they cannot be knocked overboard.

If you are starting to sail in a single-hander, many of the points above apply, although you do not have a crew to assist you. Single-handers are always best rigged on shore, ready to sail off when the boat is launched. You will often need some help when launching and recovering the boat, if only to retrieve or put away the trolley. Although the classic hove-to position (see page 51) cannot be used in a single-sail boat it can still be stopped on a close reach with the sail let out and the tiller held to leeward. In a single-handed dinghy you must concentrate on balance and trim, and practise all your movements until they are second nature. Try to sail in company until you are more experienced.

*Although experienced sailors often launch their boats with the sails hoisted, as here, beginners usually find it best to row or paddle out and hoist the sails when afloat.*

# Launching

Take a good look a the slipway, before you wheel your loaded trolley onto it to check that it doesn't end suddenly – if it does, you could fall into deep water! If the slipway is very steep or slippery, you can use a long line secured to the trolley and to a point on top of the slip, to prevent the boat and trolley running away from you. One person should pay out the rope while the other manoeuvres the trolley down the slope. When at the water's edge, stop and untie the painter from the trolley (below). Then one of you pushes the trolley into the water while the other holds the painter. As soon as the trolley is in deep enough, it is held steady while the other person floats the boat off (below). Holding the painter or the forestay, move the boat to one side of the slipway to allow other people to use it, while the other person stows the trolley. Fit the rowlocks (if you are rowing off) or get the paddle or paddles ready and then climb into the boat one at a time, the last person pushing the boat off. If you can, climb aboard the boat near the thwart and sit down rapidly in the centre to keep the weight low. The person already in the boat should balance it while the other person gets in.

*Far left, untie the painter from the trolley handle before pushing the loaded trolley into the water. Left, once the boat has been floated off from the trolley, the latter can be removed and stowed, while the other person holds the boat steady.*

# Recovery

When returning to a slipway, one person must get out before the bottom of the boat actually touches the slip. He must take care not to step out into deep water. He can then hold the boat steady while the other person collects the trolley. The boat should be moved to the side of the slip while you are waiting, to avoid causing an obstruction. Then the trolley should be pushed deep enough into the water to permit the boat to be floated onto it; never drag the boat onto the trolley or you may easily damage it. Once it is sitting correctly on the trolley, tie the painter to the trolley handle and pull the trolley up to the top of the slip, avoiding any boats being launched. With a very steep slip, use a long line from the top of the slip to the boat to act as a safety line.

*When the boat is correctly positioned on the trolley, tie the painter to the trolley handle*

*before pulling the loaded trolley out of the water.*

# Rowing

Learning to row properly takes a lot of practice and is best learned in a small rowing dinghy; a sailing dinghy is often difficult to row, owing to the windage created by the mast and rigging. If you row off from the slipway, get into the boat and sit in the middle, on the thwart, facing aft. Stretch your legs out and brace your feet. The crew should hold the boat until you are ready. Put the crutches into the fittings provided in the gunwale, with the higher arm of the crutch facing forward. Lay the oars in the crutches with the stops (if fitted) against the inboard side of the crutch. When you are ready, and the crew gets

aboard, get him to sit in the stern, and ship the rudder and tiller, so that he can steer while you row. Use the centreboard (about quarter-down) if there is a cross wind blowing. To row, lean forward with your arms extended and push your hands down to lift the blades clear of the water: then dip the blades vertically into the water and lean back, keeping your arms straight. Finish the stroke by bending your arms towards your chest. Push your hands down and forwards to lift the blades clear of the water, and lean forward again to repeat the movement.

*Left, one person rowing while the other uses the tiller to steer the boat. Right, two people rowing, with an oar each. Take care to keep the strokes in unison so that you steer a straight course.*

# Paddling

If your dinghy isn't suitable for rowing, you can use paddles. Although they are easier to stow than oars, they are not suitable for travelling long distances, or for rough conditions. If there are two of you, you can both paddle. Sit on opposite sides of the boat just aft of the shrouds, facing forwards. Hold the paddle at the top with the inboard hand, and the shaft halfway down with the other. Lean forward and dip the paddle into the water, pulling it towards the stern,

lifting the blade clear of the water before the next stroke. You both have to work in unison to steer a straight course. Alternatively, one of you can paddle while the other steers with the tiller; if on your own, you can paddle the boat from the stern. Leaning over the transom, hold the paddle vertically in the water and move the paddle from side to side, twisting the blade at the end of each stroke. Alternatively, draw the blade towards you to pull the boat along.

*Far left, using the paddle over the stern in a draw-stroke in order to pull the boat backwards through the water. Left, two people paddling over the side.*

# Returning to a weather pontoon

You will find it much easier to come alongside the part of the pontoon that lies at right angles to the weather shore rather than the part lying parallel to it. The same method is used in both cases, but in the latter requires precision timing on the part of the helmsman. If you are a novice, and have no alternative but to come alongside a pontoon parallel to the shore, then it would be advisable to lower the sails some distance off, and to paddle or row in. If the wind is at a slight angle to the shore you will find it better to approach the leeward side of the pontoon, so that the sails can flap clear of the pontoon.

*How to return to a weather shore pontoon*
*Sail towards the pontoon on a reach, and let out the sails to slow down the boat as you near the pontoon. Turn the boat into the wind to bring it to a stop alongside the pontoon. The crew should grasp the edge quickly and secure the boat.*

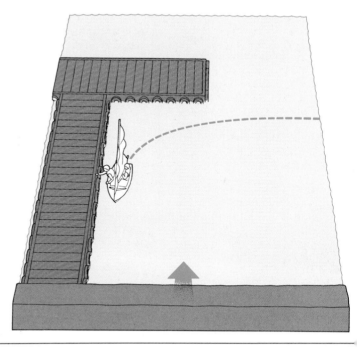

# Returning to a lee pontoon

As with a weather shore, your approach will be determined to a great extent by the position of the pontoon. You should use one method if you are planning to approach the part of the pontoon lying at right angles to the shore, and another if you are trying to come alongside the part lying parallel to the shore. Your choice may be limited by the extent of clear water around the pontoon. If in any doubt, lower the sails some distance off, and paddle or row in.

If the pontoon juts out quite a long way into the water and you have enough clear water; you can use the method shown below left. It requires careful judgment since you have to sail the boat quite close to the shore, before luffing up to stop. If you have to make your approach to the part of the pontoon lying parallel to the shore, right, you must lower the mainsail some distance from the pontoon, and come in under headsail alone.

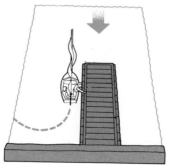

*Pontoon at right angles to the shore*
*Sail in on a broad reach, coming in close to the shore. Round the boat up head-to-wind as you approach the pontoon, and drift to a stop alongside the pontoon. The crew secures the boat in the usual way.*

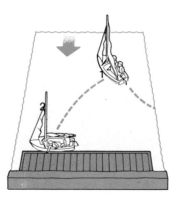

*Pontoon parallel to the shore*
*Sail to a point upwind of the pontoon, and turn the boat head-to-wind while you lower the mainsail (1). Then come in on broad reach under jib alone. As you approach let the jib flap, and drift sideways up to the pontoon edge (2), securing the boat as usual.*

## Leaving in tidal waters

As soon as you are sailing in tidal waters, you have to consider the effects of the tide, as well as the wind. You will need to be able to judge the strength of the tide (see page 98) and whether it is greater in effect than the strength of the wind, and vice versa. The strongest element will govern which side of the pontoon you leave from. As a general rule, leave from the side in the lee of the strongest element. Take particular care when a strong wind is blowing directly against the tide, as this will tend to create waves on the downtide side of the pontoon. Methods for leaving in three different wind and tide combinations are described below.

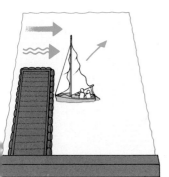

### Wind and tide together
Leave from the leeward/downtide side. Face the boat into the wind and tide, hoist the sails and lower the centreboard. To sail off, the crew backs the jib. The boat will then turn, and can be sailed off on a reach.

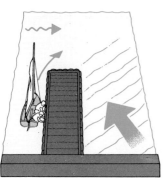

### Strong wind opposing weak tide
Leave from the leeward/uptide side. Face the boat in the direction shown, hoist the jib and lower the centre-board. Push the boat off from the pontoon and sail away under the jib alone. Hoist the main-sail in clear water.

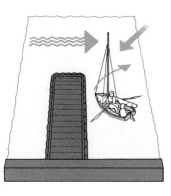

### Strong tide opposing weak wind
Leave from the windward/downtide side. Face the boat into tide, but don't hoist the sails. Push the boat off and row or paddle into clear water. Then hoist the sails and steer onto the required course.

## Returning in tidal waters

In tidal waters you should plan your return so that the boat is turned into the strongest element when coming up the pontoon. As with leaving, much depends on your ability to assess the relative strength of wind and tide. Although it is easiest to plan when the wind and tide are both in the same direction, remember that the boat will drift downtide after the sails have been lowered. The approach is more difficult when the wind and tide are opposed, making it inadvisable to come in on the windward side of the pontoon in strong winds, if there are waves. If the wind and tide are at right angles, you have a better choice of approach. You can either stop on the uptide side of the pontoon, head-to-wind, or you can stop facing into the tide on the end of it.

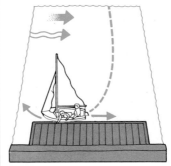

### Wind and tide together
Sail on a reach towards the shore. When near the pontoon, turn head-to-wind alongside to stop. Allow enough room to drift back with the tide.

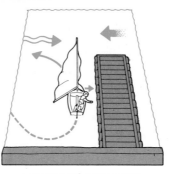

### Wind opposing tide
Approach the leeward/uptide side of the pontoon on a close reach. Tack to bring the boat alongside the pontoon. Let the sails flap and drift in sideways.

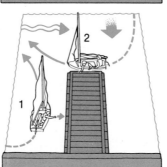

### Wind and tide at right angles
To stop on the uptide side, approach on a reach. Turn head-to-wind near the pontoon and drift in (1). To stop on the upwind side, turn head-to-wind, lower the mainsail and sail in under the jib (2).

# LEAVING AND RETURNING—MOORINGS

Moorings are more commonly used as permanent berths for cruisers and keel-boats, rather than for small dinghies, which can normally be kept on shore and launched each time they are used, without much difficulty. However, if you sail in some areas you may well need to keep your boat on moorings. In any event, you may want to moor up temporarily to a buoy while you hoist or lower sails, or stop for a picnic, for example.

Moorings are generally situated on the edge of a channel, in rivers and estuaries, laid close together to economize on space. Although the type of mooring may vary, the component parts are usually much the same – a heavy weight or anchor, known as a sinker, a length of cable or chain and a floating marker or buoy. The boat is normally secured to a rope strop attached to the chain under the buoy, or by a mooring rope tied to a ring on top of the buoy.

If your boat is kept permanently on moorings, you will need a rowing boat to get out to and back from the boat after each outing. If you are leaving the boat on a mooring for any length of time, you must secure it carefully to the mooring (see page 86) and then remove all the loose gear. Cover the boat if possible to prevent it filling with water, having checked first that the buoyancy is adequate to keep the boat afloat if it should do so.

Since moorings are close together, you must be able to sail off from, and pick up, a mooring with some degree of precision. The usual securing knot to the mooring should be exchanged for a slip line, known as singling up, so that you can leave quickly. It involves threading the boat's painter through the rope strop or the mooring ring itself, depending on the type of mooring, and securing the other end on board the boat, either to a cleat or around the mast, using a quick-release knot (see page 150). If rigged, the permanent line to the mooring buoy is dropped and the line from the boat released quickly as you sail off. An alternative method to singling up is for the crew to uncleat the line to the buoy and hold the buoy itself on board until the boat is ready to leave. You may find this

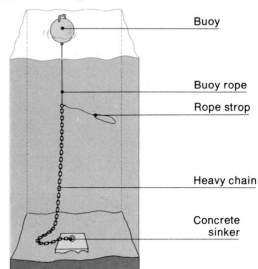

Buoy

Buoy rope

Rope strop

Heavy chain

Concrete sinker

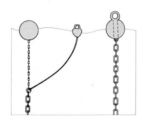

*Above left, a typical mooring with a light buoy attached by a rope to a heavy chain and sinker. Far left, a mooring with a small pick-up buoy attached by a rope line to the main chain. Left, a single buoy with a ring on top to which the boat's own mooring line can be attached.*

method is inconvenient if the crew is needed for other tasks.

When returning to a mooring, check the position of the other moored craft to see how they are lying in relation to the wind and tide. Since they will be lying bow-on to the stronger element, you can plan your own approach so that your boat also finishes up pointing into the stronger element. Always plan to pass on the downtide side of any craft moored in tidal waters, and on the downwind side of other boats in non-tidal waters. When leaving or returning to a mooring, plan your course so that you are not sailing amongst moored boats for any longer than you have to, to avoid the danger of collision. You should take great care not to sail over the lines of other boats.

*Above and left, a controlled approach to a mooring buoy is essential if the boat is to stop next to the buoy.*

# How to leave

Provided that your boat is moored in non-tidal waters, you can leave using the methods shown right. Whichever method you use, the crew should either single up the painter or release the mooring line and hold the buoy while the mainsail and jib are hoisted. When there are no obstructions, the course sailed from the mooring is not critical, but where there are, the buoy can be released at different points to control the course taken. The further aft it is released, the further from the wind you can sail off. On offwind courses, the helmsman should release the mooring.

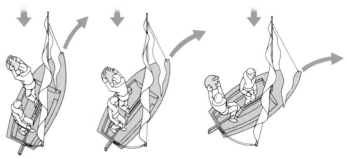

*Released at bow*
To sail away close-hauled the crew releases the buoy near the bow.

*Released amidships*
To sail away on a close reach the crew releases the buoy amidships.

*Released astern*
To sail away on a reach the helmsman releases the buoy astern.

# How to return

When returning to a mooring buoy in non-tidal waters, your approach should be as slow as possible to give the crew the best possible chance of picking up the buoy. You can usually control your speed best if you come in on a close reach, aiming to stop the boat with the mooring buoy just by the windward shroud. Let the jib flap to reduce boat speed, and ease the mainsheet if necessary to further reduce speed. The helmsman should keep the boat balanced while the crew leans out to pick up the buoy.

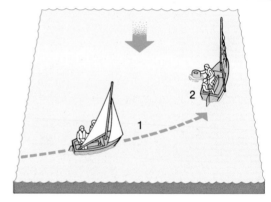

*Approach the buoy on a close reach (1). As you come in close to the mooring, ease the sails to slow down (2). The crew can pick up the mooring while the helmsman balances the boat.*

# Securing a mooring

As the boat stops close to the buoy, the crew leans over by the windward shroud and picks it up. The sails are lowered, and the mooring buoy can be made fast to the boat by leading the permanent mooring rope or strop through the bow fairlead and cleating it on deck, or around the mast. Alternatively the boat's own painter can be used to secure the buoy or, if the buoy is a small one, it can be brought on board and the rope cleated on deck.

*Right, the crew picking up the buoy*

# Leaving in tidal water

Your method of leaving in tidal water will depend on the position in which the boat is lying. If the wind and tide are opposed, the bow of the boat will face into the stronger element. If the tide is stronger, the boat will face into it, known as being "tide-rode". If the wind is stronger, the boat will face into it and is "wind-rode". If both elements are opposing and have an equal effect on the boat, it will lie at right angles to both of them, known as being "across the wind". Before preparing to leave the mooring, take a good look around and plan the course on which to sail off. In tidal waters, make sure that you pass downtide of all other boats and obstructions.

Wind-rode     Across the wind     Tide-rode

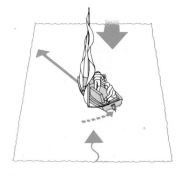

### How to leave – boat wind-rode
*A wind-rode boat presents few problems and you can hoist the mainsail without it filling. Hoist the mainsail and then the jib, lower the centreboard and drop the mooring on the windward side. Leave on a downtide course, backing the jib if necessary to sail off. When clear, steer onto the chosen course.*

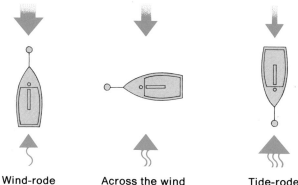

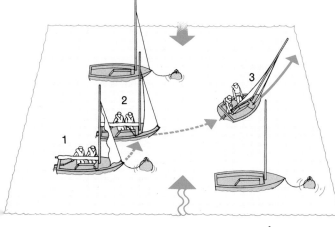

### How to leave – boat across the wind
*The most controlled method is under jib alone. Hoist the jib (1). The crew drops the mooring to leeward (2). The helmsman lowers the centreboard, and allows the boat to drift downtide, clear of any obstacles (3). Sail into clear water before hoisting the mainsail.*

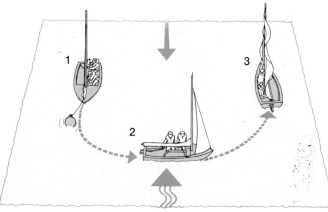

### How to leave – boat tide-rode
*If the boat is tide-rode with the wind astern, don't hoist the mainsail until the mooring has been dropped, or it will fill immediately. Hoist the jib, lower the centreboard and drop the mooring to leeward to sail off (1). Luff up (2) and hoist the mainsail before sailing off on the chosen course (3).*

# Returning in tidal water

If you are returning to a mooring in tidal water, you must assess the relative strength of the wind and tide before deciding the course on which to approach. One of the ways you can judge the strength of the tide is by looking at the mooring buoys around: a strong tidal current will produce a noticeable wake behind any object fixed in the water (right). It may help to make a dummy run before trying to pick up the mooring. If the wind and tide are in the same direction, it is usually easiest to approach from downwind of the buoy, using the method for non-tidal waters. If the tide and wind are at right angles you can use the situation to advantage by coming in from downwind and uptide of the mooring, using the tide to push you gently towards the mooring buoy. If the wind and tide are in opposition, come up to the buoy facing in the element that will have the greatest effect on the boat.

*Above, the wake on this side of the mooring buoy indicates that it is the downtide side – the more noticeable the wake, the stronger the tide.*

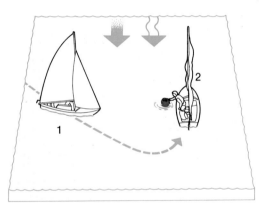

**Above, wind and tide together**
*Approach the mooring on a beam reach (1). Luff up to stop with the buoy amidships and to windward (2). Moor up in the usual way and raise the centreboard.*

**Above, wind and tide opposed**
*If the wind is stronger than the tide, approach the mooring as explained for non-tidal waters on page 86. When the tide has the most effect, sail upwind of the buoy and lower the mainsail (1). Sail up to the buoy against the tide, under jib alone (2). As soon as the painter is attached, raise the centreboard and lower the jib.*

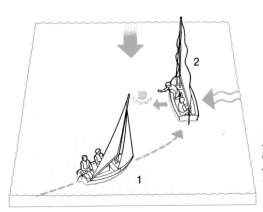

**Left, wind and tide crossed**
*Approach on a close reach, aiming uptide of the mooring, and leaving it to windward (1). As you near the mooring, luff up and allow the boat to drift downtide towards the buoy (2). Take the mainsail down quickly and raise the centreboard.*

# ANCHORING

Many people do not bother to learn the skills necessary to anchor a dinghy, regarding it as the province of cruising boats alone. Anyone who contemplates taking a boat out for a day sail on open water should always carry an anchor on board, and know how to use it. There are occasions when knowing how to anchor, and having the appropriate equipment on board, could save you a lot of trouble — for example if you want to stop for any length of time to repair a fitting on the boat, or if you are becalmed. Modern dinghies are not normally equipped with anchoring gear, but you can fit it to your boat at little extra expense.

*Dinghy at anchor.*

# Equipment

The type of anchor you carry depends on the area where you sail, as one type of anchor may not be suitable for all types of seabed. Of the four anchors shown, right, the Bruce and plough or CQR anchors will hold on most terrain. A folding grapnel is a good choice where space in the boat is limited for towage, and if the seabed in your vicinity is rocky. A mudweight is the obvious choice for estuaries or other areas where the seabed is very soft, but it will not hold on harder ground. The amount of warp you can carry in a dinghy is limited by the space available, but you must have about four times the depth of water in which you expect to anchor the boat. You can use nylon rope, which is soft and springy. There should be a cleat on the foredeck of the boat, just in front of the mast, which you can use as an attachment point for the warp, and you will need a fairlead at the bow to one side of the forestay. This fitting is essential, as it keeps the boat anchored by the bow, and prevents it shearing about when anchored. The anchor can normally be stowed on the floor of the boat just in front of the centreboard case. It should be lashed down so that it cannot move, but in a way which is easy to detach when required. The best place to stow the warp is in a bucket under the foredeck, secured to the boat. Coil the warp up and tie it with a light line to prevent the coils from tangling, before laying the warp in the bucket. Make sure that the end of the warp is tied securely to the cleat or around the mast so that the anchor and warp cannot be lost overboard.

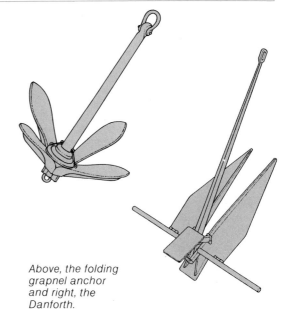

*Above, the folding grapnel anchor and right, the Danforth.*

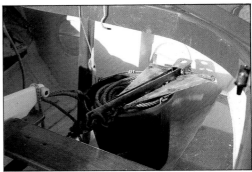

*Anchor rope stowed in bucket*

# Anchoring in non-tidal water

Where there is no tide to affect the boat, or when the strength of the tide is much weaker than the wind, you can sail up to the anchoring spot under both mainsail and jib. If you prefer, however, you can lower the jib and furl it to clear the foredeck. Having selected a suitable place to anchor, heave-to while the crew prepares the anchor and warp. Decide which tack to approach on, and then move the anchor to that side of the boat, putting it on the floor just aft of the foredeck. Lead the anchor warp outside everything through the fairlead at the bow, and back to the cleat. If your boat does not have a fairlead on the windward side, lead the warp around the forestay before passing it through the fairlead. Make sure that all the warp is free to run out when the anchor is dropped. Then sail up to the anchoring spot on a close reach, easing out the mainsail and jib, if hoisted, to slow down as you get close. When you arrive, luff gently to a close-hauled course, and let out both sails so that the boat stops. Then lower the anchor gently over the windward side, paying out the warp slowly until you feel the anchor hit the bottom; continue to pay out the warp until you have allowed for four times the depth of the water. While the crew is lowering the anchor, the helmsman should raise the centreboard fully to prevent the boat sheering about. If the anchor is holding, the boat will stop drifting back, and will lie head-to-wind. Check that it is holding by taking a transit (see page 99). Once you are certain it is, lower the mainsail (and then the jib if it has not already been lowered).

*Above, leading the warp around the forestay before passing it through the fairlead.*

*Left, the anchor being lowered gently over the side until it hits the bottom.*

# Recovering the anchor

To retrieve the anchor when the boat is lying head-to-wind, first hoist the mainsail and then fit the rudder and tiller. If possible, choose to leave on the tack that will put the bow fairlead to windward. As soon as you are ready to depart, get the crew to pull in the warp until the anchor breaks out. The boat will then have some steerage way, as it will have been pulled forward to the anchor. The helmsman can steer onto the chosen tack and sheet the mainsail in a little. The crew should take the warp out of the fairlead and continue to pull it in so that the anchor comes up on the windward side, within reach of where he is sitting, where it can be lifted aboard easily. As soon as there is room to do so, heave-to while you clean and stow the anchor and warp, and hoist the jib.

*Recovering the anchor*

# Anchoring in tidal water

Sometimes, when the effect of the tide on an anchored boat is stronger than the wind, the boat will be head-to-tide when anchored. You will tell if this is likely to be the case by looking at the way boats similar to your own are lying to their anchors or moorings. Since you must be able to stop the boat at your chosen position you will need to come up to against the tide, while still being able to let the wind out of the sails. If the wind and tide are in opposite directions, or at right angles, you must approach the anchoring spot under jib alone, or you will not be able to stop the boat sailing when the anchor goes down. When upwind of the anchoring place, prepare the gear, and then lower the mainsail, loosely stowing it before sailing up to the anchorage against the tide, under jib alone. You can slow down by letting the jib flap as you get near. The anchor is dropped as before.

If you wish to recover the anchor when the boat is tide-rode, check the wind direction. If it is coming from forward of the beam, the mainsail can be hoisted, since it will shake if let out. You can then leave as previously described. If the wind is on the beam, or from astern, you must not attempt to hoist the mainsail, but should hoist the jib instead and raise the anchor as before, sailing away under jib alone. When well clear of any obstructions, turn onto a close reach and hoist the mainsail, before heaving-to and stowing the anchor and warp.

*Coming up to the anchoring spot under jib alone, against the tide. The crew is ready to lower the anchor.*

# TOWING

Although you may not have to tow a boat very often, you should, at least, know how it is done in case the occasion arises. You also need to know how to take a tow – a fairly common occurrence, usually when the wind dies, or if you haven't succeeded in righting the boat after a capsize, for example. Normally, the towing boat will be your club rescue boat – usually a small motor launch – and in all but a flat calm sea the best solution is to be towed astern. If more than one boat needs a tow – for example if boats are becalmed in a race – then a herringbone tow will probably be used (opposite, and page 94). In an emergency, you may either have to give a tow to another sailing boat, or be towed by one yourself, usually by towing or being towed astern (overleaf).

## Towing alongside

The most convenient method for towing a boat is for it to be tied alongside the towing boat, provided the waters are reasonably calm. In large waves, the boats could easily collide and cause considerable damage to each other. Even in calm water, several fenders should be positioned along the side of the motor boat to prevent the boats touching. The sails of the boat being towed should be lowered and stowed neatly out of the way, the centreboard should be raised and the rudder and tiller unshipped. The lines securing the sailing boat to the towing boat should be secured as shown right. If the crew of the sailing boat remain aboard, their weight should be distributed on opposite sides of the boat, aft of the centreboard case. Towing a boat alongside has several advantages over towing it astern – it can be observed and kept under close control at all times, and is more manoeuvrable in confined spaces. However, the driver of the motor boat will find some difference in handling, and should take care when towing, particularly when stopping or turning.

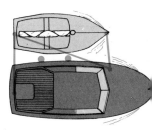

*Left and above, a sailing dinghy towed alongside a motor launch. The sails are down and stowed and the crew correctly positioned to balance the boat.*

*Right, a line of boats being towed astern. The sails should normally be lowered, as are those of the Wayfarers. However, with small boats like the Topper where the sail is fitted onto the mast in a sleeve and is difficult to lower, the best solution is to leave the sail hoisted but allow it to shake by releasing the outhaul.*

# Towing one boat astern

If the water is choppy, a boat should be towed astern rather than alongside. Every dinghy should have a good strong painter on board, which should not be less than the length of the boat. The painter should be made fast to a cleat on the foredeck or around the mast and must be fastened so it can be easily released. It must be led through a fairlead at the bow or tied by a length of line to the forestay. To take a dinghy under tow, the power boat should come alongside the dinghy once the sails have been taken down and the centreboard raised. The dinghy crew should pass the painter to the motor boat,

where it should be made fast to a tow point somewhere well forward or, failing that, to a bridle at the stern, using a bowline to fasten it (above). The helmsman should steer in the path of the towing boat, and, if there is a crew, he should sit on the opposite side, well aft.

# Towing several boats astern

If several boats are to be picked up for a tow, then each boat should drop its sails and stow them, and paddle up to join the tow. If, for any reason, this is impractical then the motor boat should move very slowly head-to-wind, while the boats sail up one by one and lower their sails when they are secured. The painter of the first boat is tied to the motor boat, and the painter of every subsequent boat to the thwart or toestraps of the boat in front. Each boat, apart from the last one in the tow, should unship the rudder and all boats must raise the centreboard. The crew should sit on opposite sides of the boat, and well aft. The last boat in the tow keeps the rudder shipped, and the helmsman steers in the wake of the tow-boat. His ability to do so will affect the manoeuvrability of the entire tow, so the most experienced helmsman should take the last position in it. In calm waters, if desired, the towing line can be shortened by making a double string of boats, from each quarter of the towing boat (right). However, the helmsman of the last boat in each string must be able to steer to keep the boats apart.

If a club motor boat is likely to be towing boats frequently, the best method to use is the herringbone tow, where the towing boat uses its own warp into which a number of loops are spliced at regular intervals at least 5m (15ft) apart. The dinghies are tied directly to the loops using their own painters, which are preferably slipped through the loop and brought back aboard the dinghy before being cleated. The dinghies take up positions alternately on either side of the rope (far right). This method has the advantage over the other of allowing dinghies to leave the tow without waiting for those behind to leave first, and it places less strain on the boats. In this method, the painter of the dinghy should not be led through the bow fairlead, and the rudder should be left on, with the centreboard partly down, because the boat has to be steered parallel to the tow-rope.

*Right, herringbone tow, with the boats fastened to a single line, on either side of it.*

*Below, towing two lines of boats astern, in calm waters. The last boats in each line keep their tillers and rudders shipped, and steer to keep the lines apart.*

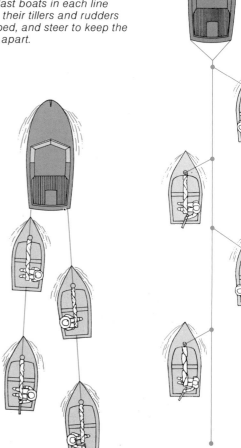

# Driving a towing boat

You should never attempt to tow a boat behind a motor boat until you are familiar with its handling characteristics, and you need to have some skill at handling the motor boat before you tow a line of boats in congested waters. It is best to have two people in the motor boat, one to steer and the other to watch the tow. If towing boats in waves, the length of the towing line must be adjusted to keep the dinghy on the front face of a wave, a couple of waves astern of the towing boat but, if several boats are being towed, the tow-rope can be shortened. With only one boat, lengthen the line when towing downwind to prevent it surfing up on the stern wave of the towing boat, and possibly crashing into it. Never try to cut in close to other boats or an obstruction. In strong cross-winds, the tow will blow away downwind, and will follow a crab-like course, so keep well to windward of any obstructions. Keep the speed down and if you find the tow unmanoeuvrable, check that the crew are sitting well aft and the centreboard of each boat is up. Make clear signals to the towed boats and, if you are towing boats in confined waters, show the code flag D (yellow and blue alternate horizontal stripes) to indicate this to any other boats.

*Right, it is always best to have two people aboard the towing boat: one person can then watch the towed boat.*

# Towing under sail

You are unlikely ever to have to tow a boat under sail, although you may have to do so in an emergency. It is very difficult to pick up a tow with both boats under sail, and one solution would be for both boats to drop their sails and make contact using paddles. In any event, the boat to be towed should lower its sails. It should leave the rudder shipped and keep the centreboard down until the painter has been fastened, as in towing one boat astern, opposite. If you do have to make contact under sail, approach the boat so that you can heave-to just ahead of and to leeward of the boat to be towed. Pass the painter over quickly and make it fast around the toestraps of your boat, having first seen that it is led through a fairlead of the towed boat or is taken once around the forestay. Start your boat moving by sheeting in. The towed boat must raise the centreboard to quarter-down, and steer in the wake of the towing boat. The crew should sit amidships, moving aft if the bows look like burying. You can tow under sail on all points of sailing, but you will not be able to point very high close-hauled. Make sure you make any changes of course clear to the towed boat, and, if you tack, get the boat moving rapidly before doing so.

# SAILING AT SEA

If you have been introduced to sailing on inland waters, the prospect of sailing at sea, on open water, is both exciting and challenging. You must learn, right from the outset, to treat the sea with respect, as it is potentially far more dangerous than confined inland waters: you can very quickly sail out of sight of land and, in the event of an emergency or accident of some kind, there may be no-one at hand to help you.

You will need to learn some new skills to deal with sailing at sea, both practical and theoretical. In practical terms you will have to deal with the effects of waves and tides, and in theoretical terms you must know what tidal conditions, if any, apply, and what weather and sea conditions to expect.

You should never go to sea without having checked the boat thoroughly, to make sure that all the equipment is present and sound, and if you are sailing alone, you should have a chart of the waters in which you are sailing and a compass, stowed in a watertight bag, secured in the boat. (If you intend sailing some way offshore, you would be advised to carry distress flares.) Always take extra clothing, a water bottle and some high-energy food, also wrapped in a waterproof container and securely stowed. Before leaving, if you intend sailing without an accompanying boat or boats, inform someone of your intended passage plan and your scheduled time of return, so that they can summon help, if necessary.

Although this may sound alarming, sea sailing is enormous fun. It allows you much more scope than you can get on most inland waters, and you will have marvellous opportunities for exploring the coastline and discovering new sailing grounds.

If your boat is large enough you can plan sailing and camping holidays exploring new parts of the coastline, having first acquired the necessary chart and tidal information. Provided you do not go out of sight of land, you can usually pilot your way around quite successfully with little knowledge of complex navigation procedures. You should understand the local buoyage system, and know how to read a chart, however, before venturing far afield.

*Setting off for a day's sailing – careful planning is a prerequisite for a successful and enjoyable trip.*

# Weather

When sea sailing, the weather conditions are all important, as you may not be able to return ashore easily if they deteriorate while you are afloat. Some knowledge of weather patterns is, therefore, a great help, and it will also make your sailing much more enjoyable. If you are racing at sea, knowing in advance what the likely changes of wind direction and strength may be could actually help you to win. While you need not understand the causes of weather variation, you must know what basic weather systems you will encounter. Most of the major dinghy-sailing areas of the world are in places where the weather is dominated by series of depressions interspersed with high pressure areas. The former bring with them strong winds, with the likelihood of major changes in wind direction, whereas the high pressure areas are associated with periods of settled weather, with light, steady winds.

Although depressions can remain stationary for some time, they usually travel fairly quickly in a west-to-east direction. Their approach is usually heralded by increasing amounts of cloud, which get gradually lower in the sky. The wind then begins to increase and to shift slowly, in a clockwise direction (in the northern hemisphere). If you suspect a depression is approaching, try to get a reliable forecast from your local meteorological office since the situation could change rapidly. A depression is usually accompanied by rain, which may well put you off the idea of sailing, even though it causes no actual problems. High pressure areas, with their settled, light winds, usually provide easier sailing conditions, since they are normally stationary for some time, and you are thus unlikely to get caught out by a rapid change of conditions.

You will often find that there are stronger breezes around the coastline during the later morning and early afternoon. Known as sea breezes, they are caused in hot weather by the sun warming up the land more than the sea, with the result that the air over the land gets hotter, expands and rises, and is then replaced by cooler air blowing in from the sea, which produces an onshore breeze. If there is no other wind, the sea breeze will blow directly onshore but if another wind is blowing, the two will combine in direction and strength. You will occasionally find this phenomenon on large stretches of water inland, with the result that there is an onshore wind blowing onto all shores of a lake with a windless area in the centre of it.

When sailing in coastal waters, you will also have to take into account the degree to which the land shelters the sea, or funnels wind onto it. Any large object upwind of you will disturb the passage of the wind and there may be a calm area in its lee or possibly an area with violent, fluctuating gusts. In light breezes, these obstructions – be they tall buildings, headlands or whatever – will cause large calm spots, while in strong winds, they will produce gusty conditions, with dramatic changes of wind direction.

In periods when high pressure is dominating the weather, you may find the conditions change in a predictable way during the course of the day. The early morning may be cloudless with light winds; as the sun rises, clouds appear and the wind increases in strength and possibly changes direction. By the afternoon the clouds may become large, even thunderous, and the wind will be at its strongest, and gusty. Then, by early evening, the clouds will clear and the wind will drop, sometimes to a calm. During the night, fog or mist may form over the sea, which will clear the next day as the sun rises. A land breeze, the opposite of a sea breeze, may develop during the night, to drop again by dawn.

# Waves

Perhaps the greatest difference between sea sailing and inland sailing lies in the formation of waves. They are produced by the friction created from the wind blowing over the surface of the water, and are largest when a strong wind has been blowing in the same direction for some time. The waves usually run roughly at right angles to the wind, and will only be really large when there is sufficient fetch (a distance of clear water over which the wind blows). They will normally be larger and steeper when the wind blows against, rather than with, a current or tidal stream (see page 99). Practice will help you trim and balance the boat to deal with the presence of waves, and techniques are given on pages 126–9. In deep water, waves do not present a great problem but when returning to or leaving from a beach in shallow water they can create problems as breaking waves may swamp the boat and even capsize it.

# Tides

The level of the sea's surface changes owing to the pull exerted upon it by the gravitational attraction of the sun and moon, and this movement is referred to as the tide. Although some places in the world have only one high and one low tide a day, there are normally two high tides and two low tides every 24 hours, with an average, in general, of about six hours between high and low water. The difference between high and low water can vary from a mere foot or so to tens of feet. Since the gravitational pull which produces the tides and the resulting tidal pattern can be calculated, you can purchase tide tables for the locality in which you are sailing, usually from a harbour master's office, a local newsagent or chandlery, which give the time and height of high and, sometimes, low water, for every day of the year. Many harbours also publish the times of high and low tides on a noticeboard near the harbour office.

If you are sailing in tidal waters, it is important to know the state of the tide before you attempt to launch the boat, since in many places it will be difficult to put the boat in the water at low tide; you might for example have to drag the boat a considerable distance up the slipway or hard, or in some areas the seabed will be mud, over which you would not be able to move the trolley. It is also equally important that you time your return to suit the state of the tide.

Since the sun and moon affect not only the height of the water but also the horizontal movement, known as the tidal stream, you need to know how this might affect you. The direction and rate of the stream are not constant, but change constantly. A local tidal atlas will give the predicted direction and rate of the stream for every hour relative to the time of local high water in the form of small charts of the area, using arrows and numbers to depict the direction and strength of the tides. There is usually one chart for each hour, from six hours before high water to six hours after it. To find out in which direction the stream is moving, and at what rate, at any particular time, you will first have to find out the time of high water locally and then work out how many hours before or after this is the time you are interested in. By turning to the relevant pages in the atlas, you can see at a glance the rate and direction of the stream, which changes hourly and is usually at its weakest at the turn of the tide, and at its strongest roughly midway between high and low water. In some places the maximum speed of the stream is only one knot or less, but in other places it can reach speeds of four knots or more. It is clearly very important that you know what these rates are, as if you are trying to return home against a foul tide, running at four knots, and your boat is only managing three knots, you are not likely to arrive! The direction of the stream usually follows the line of the coast and runs up and down estuaries and in and out of rivers. The terms "flood" and "ebb" are often used to describe the direction of flow, especially in rivers. In the period running up to high water, the stream flows into the estuaries and rivers, and is known as the flood stream. After high water, it turns around and flows out, known as the ebb stream. In confined water, the tidal stream always flows faster in deep water channels and around the outside of any bends that there may be.

A current is the term given to a flow of water moving in one direction only, sometimes with a variable rate. Currents are encountered mostly in rivers or at the mouths of them, and have a similar effect on your boat to a tidal stream.

High tide

Low tide

# Sailing in tidal waters

t is clearly vital when sailing in tidal waters to know n which direction the tidal stream is moving, and at what rate. No matter whether you are sailing with, against or across the tide, it will affect your course, or your boat speed, or both. If you are just going out for a sail around the area, aim to stay uptide of your destination so that you can return easily, even if the wind drops. Make sure that you know if the stream is going to reverse direction, by consulting your tidal atlas. When you are sailing in the same direction as he stream, you can use it to travel considerably faster, by aiming to sail, for example, where the tide s strongest: in deep water or around the outside of a bend in a river. Conversely, when sailing against

the tide, remember to keep out of areas of strong current. When sailing across a tidal stream, you may find it difficult to ensure that you sail the shortest distance. If you simply aim the boat at your destination the tide will sweep you sideways, and you will find you sail further than you need. To guard against this, you should use what is known as a transit (see below). In a tidal stream, make sure you pass fixed objects, such as moored boats, on the downtide side, so that you do not get swept onto them. In fact, you can use fixed objects to work out the direction of the stream, as the tide leaves a wake as it flows around them. The size of the bow wave it creates will give you some idea of its strength.

# Using a transit

To take a transit to check your course, you should line up two fixed objects – say a buoy off your destination and a prominent object on the shore behind. You should then steer the boat to keep the two objects constantly aligned. With a tidal stream running across your course, you will find that you have to steer off to one side, and point the bow uptide of the objects. The effect of the tidal stream will be such that the boat moves in a crab-like

fashion in relation to the seabed, although you travel in a straight line to arrive at your destination. You don't necessarily have to use objects in front of you for a transit, you could just as easily use a transit astern. You can also use objects not in line with each other, provided you keep their relationship to each other constant. You can also use a transit to provide a clearing line in order not to hit a charted obstruction at a harbour mouth, for example.

*The rock is to the right of the cliff edge. To bring them in transit you must steer to the right.*

*The rock is now in transit with the cliff edge.*

*The rock is now to the left of the cliff edge and to bring it back in transit you must steer to the left.*

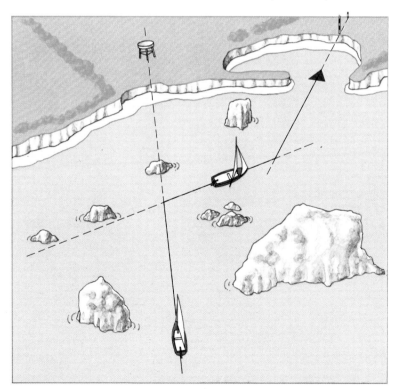

# Choosing a route

Don't be too ambitious for your first day's sail. Choose a destination where you can stop for a lunch break after you have been sailing for a couple of hours, assuming a Force 3 (7–10 knots). Make sure that your chosen destination has some amenities where you can have a meal and a drink. Check in advance whether the owner or manager has any objection to your arriving in wet sailing gear. You should always have an alternative passage plan for a closer destination, just in case the wind either drops or increases, making it difficult for you to reach your first choice. Before you leave, have a look at a large-scale chart of the area, which shows both departure point and destination, and find out if there are any obvious hazards, such as busy shipping channels, en route. Work out a passage which will avoid any such dangers, and try to sail in

sheltered waters wherever possible, bearing in mind the likely direction in your area of any strong winds that might blow up. If you are sailing in tidal waters, examine the tide tables for the area thoroughly, and note the times of high and low waters for the day, with their respective heights. Then look in the tidal atlas to check the direction of the stream during the time you are planning to be afloat. Try to ensure that the stream is running in the same direction that you wish to travel, or, if not, that it is across your course rather than in opposition to it. Don't try to sail against the stream for any distance unless its rate is less than one knot; in light winds, you may find it difficult to make much headway even then. You may have to reconsider your projected trip and rearrange your time of departure or your choice of destination.

# Preparing the boat

Assuming that your boat is in good general condition you should only need to give it a final check — mainly over areas such as the standing and running rigging, and the sails and rudder — to ensure that it is all in order. You should aim to be as self-sufficient as possible, as there will be no rescue boat in close attendance. You should equip the boat with an anchor and warp of a suitable size for the boat (see page 89). You should also include a simple first-aid kit containing aspirin or paracetomol; elastoplast; sterile dressing; bandages; anti-seasickness tablets;

antiseptic cream; sunburn lotion and scissors. Take a small flare pack with you, and a knife, a screwdriver, pliers, assorted lengths and sizes of spare line, spare shackles, nuts and bolts, spare clothing, food and drink, a sailbag or reefing strop, and oars and crutches, or paddles. The foregoing seems like a formidable list of equipment but in practice it can easily be stowed in most dinghies suitable for daysailing. Make sure that everything is packed in waterproof containers, and tied into the boat. Always wear your buoyancy garments.

*A Wayfarer setting out for a day's sail has a reefed mainsail, in expectation of fresher winds when out on open water.*

# Forecasts

A couple of days before your proposed trip, take note of the weather reports for the area you are interested in. You can get them from your local television station weather reports, from the national and local newspapers, from the recorded telephone service, radio bulletins, or by making a call to the coastguard, harbour master of your local weather centre. You can build up a picture of the current situation which will help you to assess the likely weather on the day in question. On the day of your trip, phone up your local weather centre and speak to the duty forecaster. Tell him your plans and ask for any weather information that may help you. Note his forecast and listen to any advice he can give. Then decide whether the proposed trip is feasible. If the wind is likely to be very light or strong, or if the visibility is poor, your plans will probably have to

change. Never stick to any plan if the omens are bad; you would be much better to rearrange it than run unnecessary risks. If you have made the decision to go, inform the coastguard, harbour master or some other responsible person of your exact plan, route, destination and expected time of return. Check in when you return, and, if you change your plans, make sure that the appropriate people are told of the changes.

| Beaufort scale | Wind strength in knots | Land signs | Dinghy criteria |
|---|---|---|---|
| 0 | Calm less than 1 | Smoke rises vertically. Leaves do not stir. | Drifting conditions. Heel the boat to reduce the wetted surface and enable the sails to assume an aerofoil shape. Make no sudden movements. |
| 1 | Light airs 1–3 | Smoke drifts. Wind vanes do not respond | Sufficient to maintain gentle forward motion. Sails should be flattened. Crew balance boat to keep it slightly bow down and heeled to leeward. |
| 2 | Light breeze 4–6 | Wind felt on the face. Leaves rustle. Light flags not extended. Wind vanes respond. | Sufficient to sail at an even speed with the boat upright. Sails can be full but must be adjusted to changes in wind speed and direction. |
| 3 | Gentle breeze 7–10 | Light flags extended. Leaves in constant motion. | Most dinghies will sail at hull speed. Planing possible for thoroughbred dinghies. Ideal conditions for learners. |
| 4 | Moderate breeze 11–16 | Most flags extend fully. Small branches move. Dust and loose paper may be raised. | Crew fully extended. Planing on most points of sailing. A learner's gale – make for shore. |
| 5 | Fresh breeze 17–21 | Small trees in leaf sway. Tops of all trees in noticeable motion. | Ideal sailing conditions for experienced sailors. Capsizing common amongst the more inexperienced crews. |
| 6 | Strong breeze 22–27 | Large branches in motion. Whistling heard in wires. | Dinghy sailor's gale. Often difficult to make progress without reefing. Only experienced crews race. |
| 7 | Near gale 28–33 | Whole trees in motion. Inconvenience felt when walking against wind. | Most dinghies remain on shore. Those which go afloat risk gear failure and being overpowered. |
| 8 | Gale 34–40 | Twigs broken off trees. Generally impeded progress on foot. Rarely experienced on land. | Dinghies should be securely tied down to prevent them blowing over. |

# STOWING

If you want to save on maintenance, you must stow your boat and its equipment properly after sailing. You should wash the boat and sails down with fresh water (particularly if you have been sailing in sea water), and allow the sails to dry before packing them away.

Whether you leave the rudder and other equipment in the boat depends on where you keep your boat. Removing the sails is a simple exercise – you simply have to reverse the rigging procedure. Make sure that the halyards are tied away from the mast so that they don't frap and that any loose equipment in the boat is securely tied down. Inspection hatches and bungs should be left open to allow air to circulate and any water to drain away. The boat should be properly covered and tied down.

*Covered dinghies in a boat park.*

# Folding the mainsail

You will find it difficult to make a neat job of folding the mainsail unless you lay it flat on the ground first. Make the folds towards the wind to prevent them blowing back. It is best if two of you work together on either side of the sail. Don't forget to remove the battens first, and stow them in the sailbag.

**1** *Starting at the foot of the sail, make your first fold about 1 m (3ft) from the foot.*

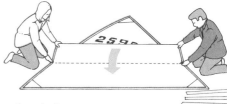

**2** *Make another similar-sized fold near the head and lay it on the first.*

**3** *Continue folding until the whole sail is neatly in place.*

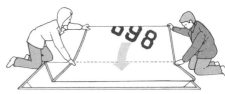

**4** *Make sure the sail is smooth and crease-free.*

**5** *Start to fold the sail across. Fold it over and over until it is small enough to fit in the bag, but avoid tight folds.*

# Rolling the jib

Because the jib has a wire reinforcement, you should roll rather than fold it, to prevent distortion. Where possible, remove the sheets from the sail.

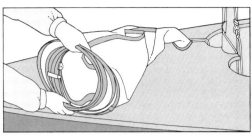

**1** *Start to coil the wire luff at the jib head.*

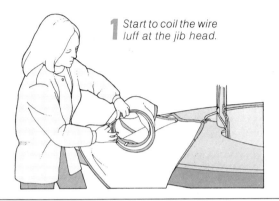

**2** *Continue rolling until the jib forms a neat coil. Smooth out any creases as you roll it.*

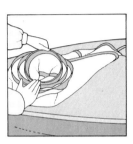

**3** *Lay the coiled luff on the sail and fold the sail loosely before stowing it in the bag.*

# Stowing the boat

Small sailing boats are usually kept on land when not being used. How you store your boat depends to some extent on its type and where you keep it. Very small boats can be kept on racks which save space and give good protection. Larger boats are usually stored on their launching trolleys with the bows supported on a trestle, or on several old tyres for example, to allow water or condensation to drain out. Always cover the boat with a good waterproof cover, which should be tied down securely onto chocks.

*Covering the boat*
*This dinghy is properly covered, fastened to the ground on chocks at the sides and supported at the front on a trestle to allow any moisture to drain out of it.*

*A special trolley and trailer combination designed to support a racing keel boat.*

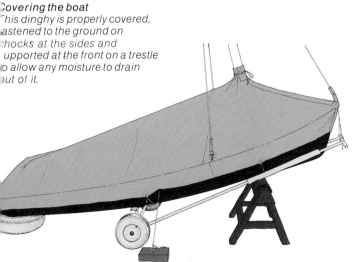

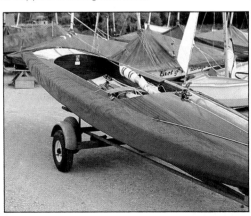

*An under-cover used to protect the hull.*

# CAR-TOPPING AND TRAILING

If you keep your boat at home, or some distance from the water, you will have to trail it each time you sail. Even if you keep it at a boat park near the water's edge, you will probably have to move it now and again by road. You have the option, if the boat is particularly light and small, of being able to carry it on the roof of the car if you prefer. In either case you will have to have special equipment fitted to the car – either a strong tow bar of the ball-and-socket or drop-pin type if you are trailing, or a robust roof-rack, preferably of the type which has two bars across the roof of the car, fitted to the guttering with clamps. If you are trailing the boat you will of course need a roadworthy trailer which will carry your boat properly, and a lighting board for the back of the trailer which can be wired up to the lighting system of the car. If the boat is a particularly heavy one, the regulations may stipulate that you have an over-run braking system for the trailer, and you should contact your local highway authority to find out what is required.

Whichever method you use, the boat must be secured properly, so that it will not slip off the roof-rack or trailer. If car-topping the boat, make sure that the roof rack is padded with rubber to absorb any shocks and prevent the boat being damaged. Always obey the traffic regulations as regards speed when trailing, and make sure that any ancillary equipment is tied down securely.

## Loading the boat

The boat is usually carried upside-down so that its sides rest firmly on the bars of the roof racks. If the boat has to be carried the right way up for any reason, the hull must be properly supported and it must either be covered or the bungs must be left out to prevent it filling with rainwater. The boat is carried with the bow facing forwards and should be secured to the roof racks by tie-down straps or ropes lashed across its width. It is also essential to tie the bow and the stern to the car bumpers to prevent the boat lifting off at speed. The mast and boom are tied to the roof racks separately. Plenty of padding should be taped to the bars and ropes to prevent any damage to the boat.

Loading the boat – one person

**1** *Place the boat on the ground and lift the bow so that it rests on the rear rack.*

**2** *Lift the stern and push the boat forward onto the front rack, and then tie the boat down securely.*

Loading the boat – two people

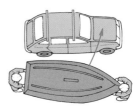

*One person should hold the bow and the other the stern, and the boat should then be lifted onto the roof from the side. Move the stern into position first.*

# Trailing a boat

Road trailers come in two basic forms, as an A-frame construction or as a B-frame one. Both types operate in more or less the same way by supporting the boat on specially shaped chocks or rubber rollers and providing a cup-shaped support for the mast when it is lying horizontally on top of the boat. The A-frame trailer can often be adjusted to accommodate different sizes of boat, and has a strong central supporting strut. The B-frame type, while not usually adjustable, can be combined with a launching trolley so that the boat can be moved on its trolley directly onto the trailer, thus avoiding any heavy lifting. The trolley is self-stowing on the trailer and locks in position. Whichever type you use, you must fix a lighting board to the rear, conforming to the appropriate road safety regulations. With heavier boats, such as a large day boat, an over-run braking system should be fitted to the trailer and you should consult a trailer manufacturer about a suitable type.

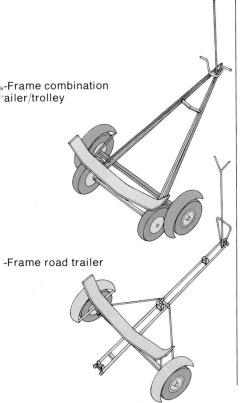

A-Frame combination trailer/trolley

B-Frame road trailer

# Loading the trailer

You will usually find it easier to load the trailer if it is already attached to the towing vehicle, since this will help to stabilize it. If you are loading the boat directly onto a trailer, without a trolley, you will need two or more people, depending on the weight of the boat, to lift the boat onto the supporting chocks. Once loaded, tie the boat down carefully with straps or ropes to prevent it shifting. Loading a boat already stowed on a trolley is much simpler.

**Loading onto a combination trailer**

**1** *Pull the trolley forward behind the trailer in line with the loading rollers.*

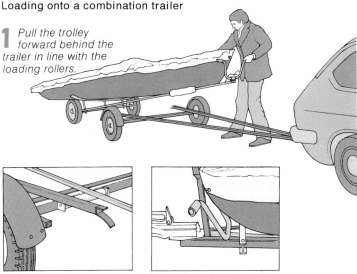

**2** *Then pull the trolley far enough forward to allow the trolley axle to lock into the supporting brackets.*

**3** *Lower the trolley handles until the trolley and trailer can be clamped together.*

# Preparing for the road

Place the mast in the mast-support so that the heel rests on the aft decking or against the inside of the transom. Tape the shrouds and the halyards to the mast and pad the mast heel to prevent damage to the boat. Tie the mast to the support and to the central thwart. Remove or secure all loose equipment inside the boat. Fix the lighting board in place and connect it to the car socket. Check that the towing coupling is locked and the safety chain attached.

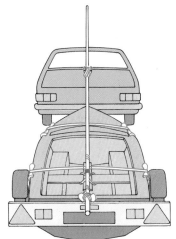

# RULES OF THE ROAD

As with any other form of traffic, sailing boats must obey certain rules to prevent collisions occurring. The rules are internationally agreed and were revised in 1972. Their full title is the International Regulations for Preventing Collisions at Sea, and they are available in booklet form or in the many nautical almanacs published. The regulations are usually referred to, briefly, as the rules of the road.

As the helmsman of a small sailing boat, you must realize that you have as much responsibility as the captain of a large tanker, for example, and if a collision occurs as a result of your failing to observe the rules, prosecution could well follow. Although there is a basic rule that power gives way to sail it only applies when the powered boat has freedom to manoeuvre. It would be foolhardy for a small boat to stand on its rights when on a collision course with a large powered boat. However, any change of course you make must be carried out in plenty of time so that the skipper of the other vessel is aware of your intentions.

The three main rules that apply to sailing boats meeting are shown below, but you should have a copy of the regulations for more detailed information on the less common ones.

*Right, the port tack boat is crossing ahead of the starboard tack one, having calculated that there is enough room to do so safely. If a collision were to occur, the port tack boat would be held responsible.*

# Rights of way

In order to understand the rules, you need to know when your boat is on port tack and when it is on starboard tack: port tack is when the wind blows over the port side and starboard tack is when the wind blows over the starboard side. If you have difficulty remembering, put stickers with "port" and "starboard" marked on them on the appropriate sides of the boom. If you are in any doubt about your rights, aim to pass behind another boat and not in front of it. The three basic rules for sailing boats on a collision course are given here.

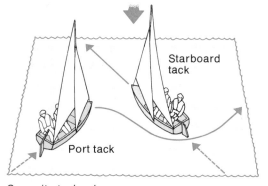

**Opposite tack rule**
*If two boats are on opposite tacks, the port tack boat must keep clear of the starboard tack boat.*

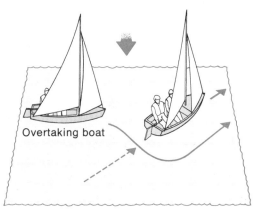

**Same tack – overtaking rule**
*If two boats are on the same tack the overtaking boat must keep clear.*

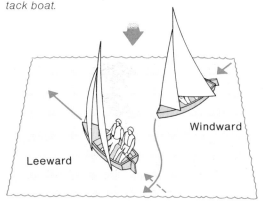

**Same tack – windward rule**
*If two boats are on the same tack, the boat to windward must keep clear of the leeward boat.*

# INCREASING BOAT SPEED

Once you have mastered the basic techniques of handling a standard sailing dinghy, you may well wish to try out your skills in a faster boat, such as a high-performance racing dinghy. Modern racing boats are light, responsive and considerably less stable than the heavier family dinghies, but are considerably faster on all points of sailing. They usually incorporate a range of equipment designed to get the best possible speed out of the boat, in particular a trapeze system, which enables the crew to gain more righting power by shifting his weight further outboard, and a spinnaker system, which enables you to set an additional loose-footed sail on offwind course. A modern high-performance boat like the 470, opposite, would be suitable for someone wishing to progress to a faster and more exciting boat.

To get the best out of your boat you will have to sharpen up your reactions and improve your judgment, apart from learning how to use the trapeze and how to fly a spinnaker. You will need to be able to handle your boat properly in waves and in rougher weather, and you will also need to know how to induce the boat to plane (rise up on its own bow wave and skim across the water). Boat speed can also be improved by adjusting the rig to suit different wind conditions (see pages 142–5).

# Planing

The secret of getting a boat to plane lies in the helmsman's ability to anticipate a gust of wind before it strikes. He should start to bear away as he sees a gust approach, and ease out the sheets to balance the crew weight and heeling force, so that the boat is sailing upright. As soon as the bow begins to lift, the crew and helmsman should both move aft, keeping the boat trimmed level. As boat speed increases, the sails should be sheeted in to allow for a shift in the apparent wind and, when the gust passes, the boat can be held on the plane by luffing slightly to keep the apparent wind speed constant. If the boat begins to come off the plane, it may help to move the crew weight further forward.

*Right, with the boat upright, the crew well aft and the sheets eased slightly, as a gust hits, it should not be difficult to plane away under perfect control.*

# The racing dinghy

A modern racing dinghy usually has a number of features which distinguish it from a family one. The hull is generally of lighter-weight material, as are all the fittings. The mainsheet system is usually a centre one, with multi-purchase blocks to cope with the extra power produced by a larger sail area. A trapeze system and spinnaker equipment is normally incorporated, and refinements to the kicking strap, centreboard and jib fairleads give a greater degree of control and flexibility.

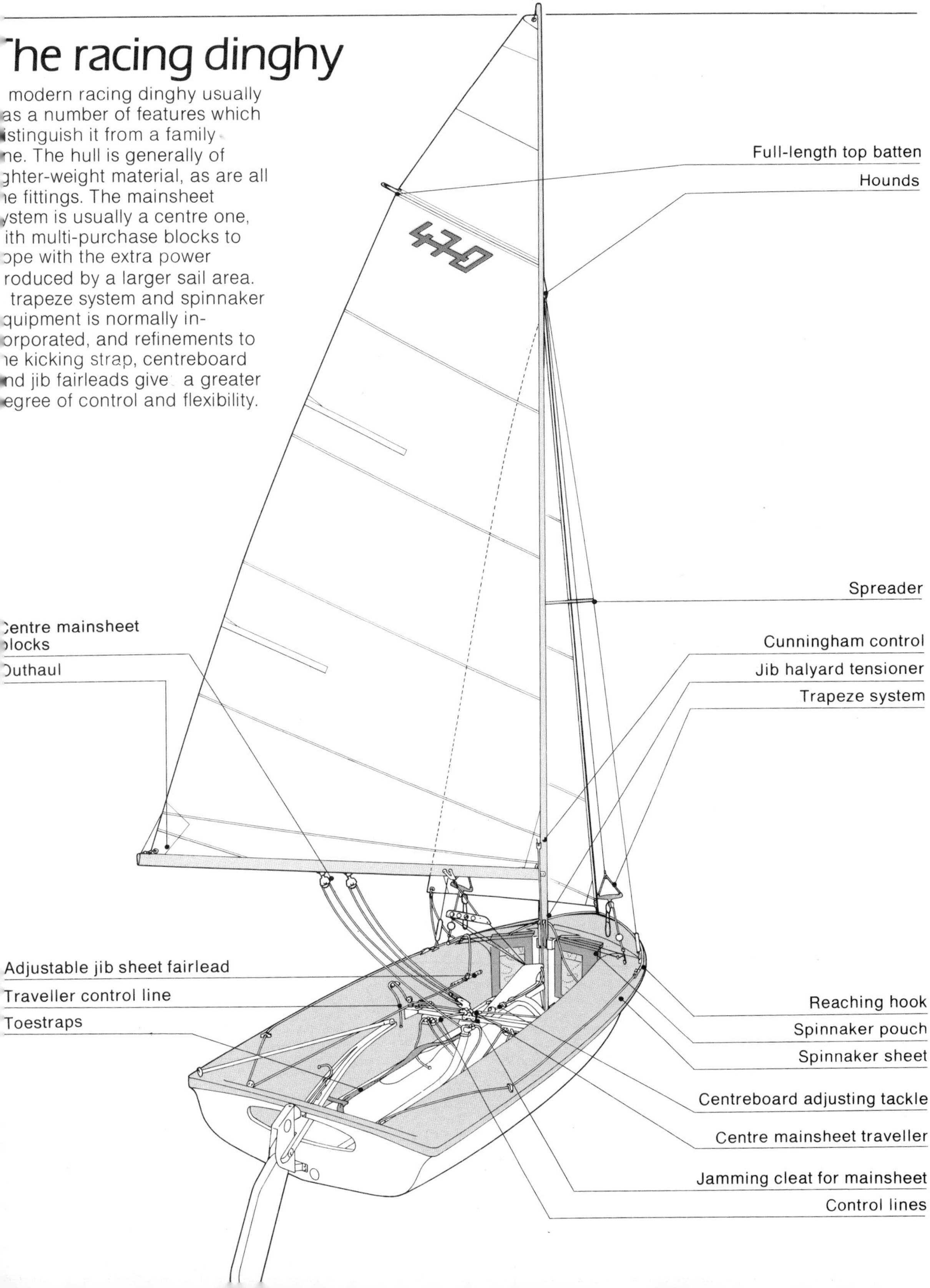

Full-length top batten

Hounds

Spreader

Cunningham control

Jib halyard tensioner

Trapeze system

Centre mainsheet blocks

Outhaul

Adjustable jib sheet fairlead

Traveller control line

Toestraps

Reaching hook

Spinnaker pouch

Spinnaker sheet

Centreboard adjusting tackle

Centre mainsheet traveller

Jamming cleat for mainsheet

Control lines

# SPINNAKERS

A spinnaker provides extra driving power for the boat on offwind courses. Although the original spinnakers were designed for use only on downwind courses, modern spinnakers have been constructed for use on a much broader range of points of sailing.

Unlike the other sails, the spinnaker is not attached along the length of the luff to a spar or stay. The construction of the spinnaker can vary considerably (see below) and there is a range of types to choose from, depending on your needs. The equipment required for a spinnaker system consists of a sheet and guy to control the clews of the sail, a spinnaker pole, which acts in a similar manner to the boom and is fixed to the mast and to one clew of the sail, a spinnaker halyard to hoist and lower the sail, and an uphaul/downhaul system to support the pole. A number of modern boats have a special stowage system for the spinnaker in the shape of a chute, which makes hoisting and lowering much simpler, but the majority of boats have a simple pouch into which the spinnaker is packed after lowering.

Handling a spinnaker demands some skill on the part of both helmsman and crew. The helmsman has to be able to steer the boat to keep the spinnaker flying and the crew must be able to hoist, lower and trim the sail efficiently. The following pages show the techniques for spinnaker handling, but spinnaker work is best learned under the guidance of an experienced sailor, as not only is it easy to get the sail into a tangle when hoisting and lowering, but it exerts a considerable pull once hoisted, and an inexperienced crew may well find it unmanageable even in moderate winds.

# Spinnaker construction

The very first spinnakers were assymetric sails, something like a baggy genoa in appearance, boomed out on a long pole. By the 1930s a symmetrical sail, more or less like the spinnaker as we know it today, had been developed for use on six-metre boats. Cotton was used for these early sails but was of course heavy and difficult to handle and by the 1950s nylon had been introduced, which was much lighter and more resilient. Developments in spinnaker cut in recent years have produced a number of different designs and new materials have also been introduced. On dinghies, the most common types of spinnaker are the horizontal, radial-head and tri-radial cuts, right. Which type you choose depends partly on the type of boat and partly on the conditions you will be sailing in. The horizontal cut is used principally for light-weather or small spinnakers and the radial head and tri-radial cuts tend to be used for larger spinnakers.

**Horizontal cut**
*Horizontal cut spinnakers stretch mainly at the head. These are best used downwind only.*

**Radial head**
*A light weather sail for all-round use, the radial head combines the radial and horizontal cuts.*

**Tri-radial**
*This spinnaker combines the radial and horizontal cuts to produce an ideal all-purpose sail.*

Limited stretch

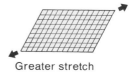

Greater stretch

**Spinnaker cloth**
*Spinnaker cloth must be light but not so elastic that it stretches easily. The nylon cloth above is designed to stretch only on the cross. Other materials, like Polyant and Dynac, are also commonly used and have stretch-resistant properties.*

# Parts of the spinnaker

Apart from the spinnaker itself, you will need the appropriate ancillary equipment, such as a spinnaker pole, a halyard and hoisting system, and sheets, sheet leads and cleats, to control the set of the spinnaker. You will also need some form of stowage system for the sail. The spinnaker pole is attached to the windward sheet, which is then referred to as the guy. Most boats have a continuous sheet system, as shown right, in which each end of it is attached to a clew.

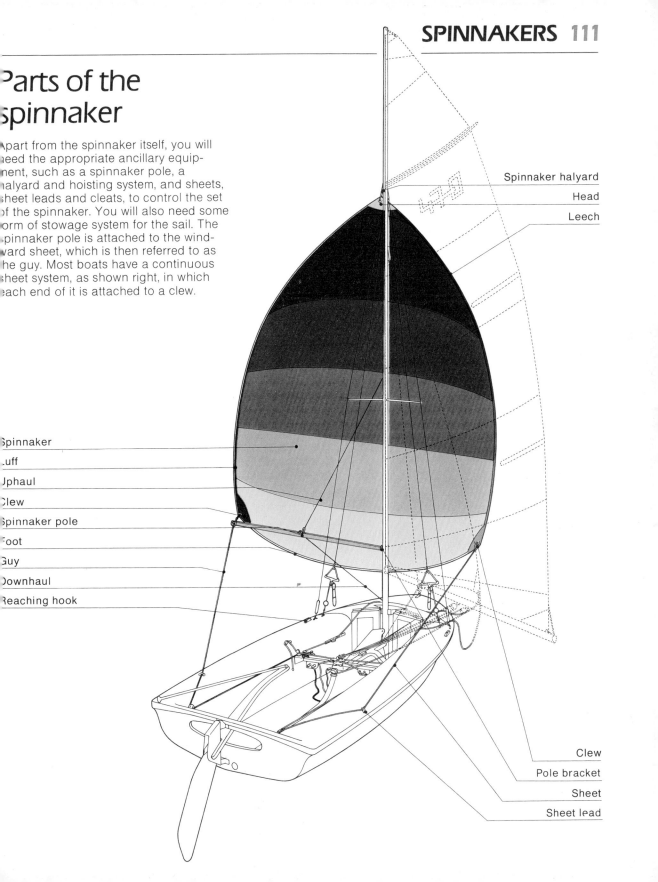

Spinnaker halyard

Head

Leech

Spinnaker

Luff

Uphaul

Clew

Spinnaker pole

Foot

Guy

Downhaul

Reaching hook

Clew

Pole bracket

Sheet

Sheet lead

# Spinnaker pole

A removable spar, the spinnaker pole, is used to
support the windward clew of the spinnaker. An
uphaul/downhaul system is fitted to the mast, as is a
bracket onto which one end of the pole can be fitted.
The spinnaker pole normally has quick-release
fittings at each end which enable the crew to fasten
the pole to the mast at the inboard end, and to the
spinnaker guy at the outboard end. The hook
attached to the uphaul/downhaul system is fitted to
the eye on the upper side of the pole, and its
position can be altered to raise or lower the pole
height. Correctly fitted, the quick-release fittings on
the pole should have the openings uppermost, as
shown below.

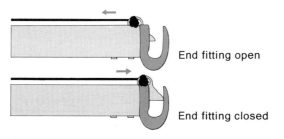

End fitting open

End fitting closed

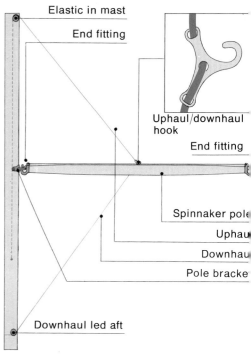

Elastic in mast

End fitting

Uphaul/downhaul hook

End fitting

Spinnaker pole

Uphau

Downhau

Pole bracke

Downhaul led aft

# Pole height

Once the spinnaker has been
hoisted, the pole height will
need adjustment to get the
sail to set well. The two clews
of the sail should be parallel,
and the pole must be raised
or lowered to bring them into
line. Generally, in moderate
winds, the pole should be
approximately at right angles
to the mast. If the pole is either
too high or too low, the sail
will not set correctly and will
not have its full driving force.

Pole set correctly

Pole too high

Pole too low

*Above, on a close
reach the pole can
be raised to move the
spinnaker up and
away from the
mainsail and jib.*

*Right, a perfectly set
spinnaker on a 505
sailing on a broad
reach.*

# Pouch system

If your dinghy has a pouch stowage system for the spinnaker, there will be two fabric pouches, one on each side of the mast (right), which are closed by flaps secured with a shock cord. The spinnaker is hoisted directly from whichever pouch it happens to be stowed in. This means that it is vital that the spinnaker itself is free of twists and that the head and both clews are at the top of the pouch so they can be fastened quickly and easily.

*This 470 has a spinnaker pouch either side of the mast. Each pouch has a top flap closed by shock cord.*

# Packing the spinnaker

With a pouch system, you must always make sure that the spinnaker is properly packed, because otherwise any attempt to hoist the spinnaker will meet with failure. It is extremely easy to get twists in the spinnaker and so the packing routine must be fully understood and should be practised ashore before attempting to hoist the sail afloat. The best method is to put the boat on the trolley head-to-wind, with no other sails rigged, and hoist the spinnaker which an experienced person has already packed properly. To hoist the sail, attach the halyard to the head of the spinnaker and the sheets to the clews. You will need two people – one to lower the sail and the other to pack it. The first person should lower the halyard slowly while the other takes the windward clew and working along the windward luff gathers it into the pouch, keeping the windward clew out, and also the head of the sail when it is reached. The remainder of the sail can then be bundled into the pouch, with the clews and head emerging from the top of it. If the sail is going to be hoisted again immediately, the halyard is normally left rigged, and fastened under the reaching hook to prevent it flogging.

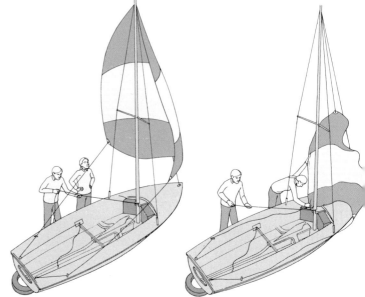

**1** *Having hoisted the spinnaker without twists, one person should start to lower the sail by releasing the halyard.*

**2** *The other person takes the windward clew and gathers the luff into the pouch leaving the windward clew and head out. The remainder of the sail is then bundled into the pouch.*

**3** *The two clews and the head are left out of the pouch, and the halyard is fastened under the reaching hook if the spinnaker is to be hoisted again immediately.*

# Chute system

any high-performance dinghies have a chute towage and hoisting system fitted. With this system, ne spinnaker is stowed in a fabric sock or tube nder the foredeck, which has a glass reinforced lastic opening either in front of or to the side of the orestay. As the spinnaker is hoisted it emerges from ne foredeck opening. The chute system has several dvantages: the spinnaker cannot twist because it is ulled directly into the sock from the centre of the oinnaker, and it is quick and easy to operate. owever, the opening in the foredeck does allow ater to get into the boat and can cause friction on e sail.

he spinnaker is hoisted by the halyard, which is ttached to the head of the sail and led back from e mast to a jamming cleat near the helmsman. nis halyard then continues through the sock or ıbe, and is fastened to the spinnaker in one of two ositions to form the downhaul. When the halyard ttached to the head is released and the downhaul ulled, the spinnaker collapses and is pulled ırough the tube.

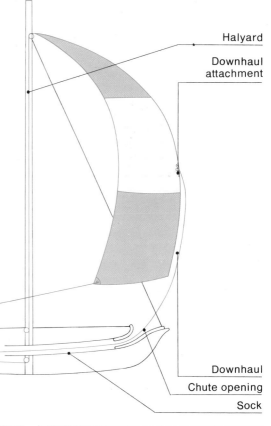

Halyard

Downhaul attachment

Downhaul

Chute opening

Sock

Jamming cleat

*Above and left, the chute system on a Fireball. Chute systems are most commonly found on racing dinghies as they enable the spinnaker to be hoisted rapidly.*

# Hoisting and lowering

The best course on which to hoist or drop a spinnaker is a broad reach. Cleat the mainsheet and jib sheet first, and check that the halyard is not fouled, and the sheets attached and correctly led outside the shrouds and the forestay. The crew and the helmsman both have to carry out their normal sailing duties while hoisting and lowering a spinnaker, so the helmsman must be able to steer the boat standing up, with the tiller between his knees, to leave his hands free to control the spinnaker.

*Flying Dutchmen sailing downwind under spinnaker during a race.*

# Leeward pouch hoist

Hoisting a spinnaker from a pouch on the leeward side of the boat is a great deal easier than trying to hoist it on the windward side, so whenever you can, you should use this method. Being able to do so will, of course, depend on whether the spinnaker has been stowed in the appropriate pouch. The helmsman should steer the boat onto a broad reach, and the crew should remove the halyard from under the reaching hook, where it is normally stowed.

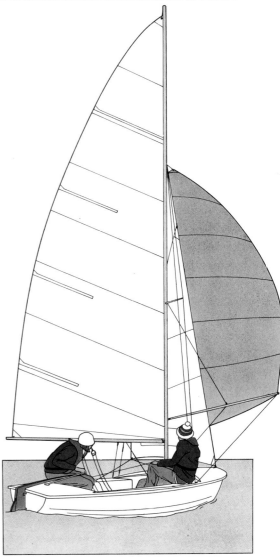

**1** *The crew clips the pole to the guy and attaches the uphaul and downhaul to the pole.*

**2** *The crew fits the pole to mast while helmsman pulls on the halyard to hoist the spinnaker, and takes control of sheet and guy to set the sail. The crew sits on the windward side of the boat and clips the guy under the reaching hook before cleating it.*

**3** *The crew then takes control of the sheet. The helmsman sits down to balance the boat and steers onto the required course while the crew plays the spinnaker (see page 120).*

# Windward pouch hoist

To hoist the spinnaker successfully on the windward side of the boat, both helmsman and crew must operate as a team and the boat should be sailed onto a broad reach prior to the hoist. Much depends on good timing and correct preparation. Before you start a windward hoist, the helmsman must place the spinnaker pole where the crew can pick it up easily. The guy must be cleated in the appropriate position (see Marking the sheets, page 120) and the usual checks made that the spinnaker is ready to hoist.

**1** Having removed the spinnaker from the windward pouch, the crew holds it tightly bundled in one hand, in front of the shroud on the windward side, and keeps the sheet in the other hand. The helmsman takes in any slack on the halyard, steering the boat with his knees.

**2** The crew throws the sail up and forwards to clear the forestay, shouting "Hoist". The helmsman hoists the sail rapidly and the crew pulls on the sheet to pull it to leeward. While the helmsman keeps the sail full, the crew fits the pole to the guy, attaches the uphaul/downhaul and fits the pole to the mast. Helmsman and crew sit down to balance the boat and the crew takes control of the sheet.

# Chute systems

The chute system is easier to use than a pouch one, since it is situated in the centre of the bow. To hoist the spinnaker, the crew should first cleat the sheets in the marked positions (see page 120). The helmsman can then hoist the spinnaker and keep it full while the crew attaches the uphaul/downhaul to the pole, and the pole to the spinnaker guy and mast. To lower the spinnaker, the crew should keep the foot of the sail pressing against the jib luff, as the helmsman pulls on the downhaul. When the sail enters the chute, the crew releases the guy and sheet and detaches the spinnaker pole from the mast.

# Lowering to pouch

You can lower the spinnaker to windward or to leeward with a pouch stowage system. The windward drop is the easiest because the crew weight is on the windward side of the boat throughout, balancing it much more effectively. You should only use the leeward drop if you need to have the spinnaker packed in that pouch ready for a future leeward hoist. Try to carry out the drop as fast as possible to prevent the sail tangling.

**Leeward drop**
The helmsman steers onto a broad reach. The crew then uncleats the guy and, as the helsman releases the halyard, takes the clew in under the boom and jib, and packs the sail. The pole is then taken down from the mast and the uphaul/downhaul detached.

**Windward drop**
Helmsman steers on to a broad reach and uncleats the halyard. The crew unclips the spinnaker pole from the mast, removes the uphaul/downhaul and unclips the pole from the guy. The crew then pulls the sail down by the luff and packs it.

# Gybing

Gybing a boat with the spinnaker set is a fairly skilled task, which requires team-work and practice by both helmsman and crew. The helmsman has to be able to steer the boat with the tiller between his knees, so that his hands are free to control the sheet and guy, as it is his job to keep the spinnaker set and under control, and the boat balanced, through-out the gybe. The crew should be free to concentrate on unclipping the pole from one side of the boat, and re-clipping it on the other. To prepare for the gybe, the helmsman should steer the boat onto a run and check that his course is clear. The crew should then adjust the guy to bring the pole to an angle of about 45° to the centreline of the boat, in order to set the spinnaker squarely across the bow of the boat (see Marking the sheets, page 120). The crew should then release the guy from the reaching hook, and cleat both it and the sheet. The boat is then ready to be gybed in the usual way.

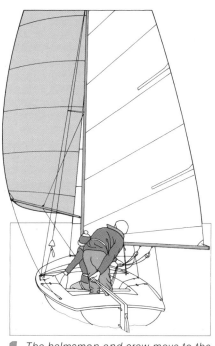

*Right, it is very important to keep the spinnaker full, and under control, during the gybe if boat speed is to be maintained.*

**1** *The helmsman and crew move to the centre of the boat and gybe the boat, pulling the mainsail and jib onto the new leeward side.*

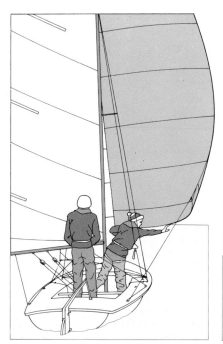

**2** *The crew unclips the pole from the mast only and clips that end to the new guy, while the helmsman keeps the sail set and balances the boat.*

**3** *Pushing the pole out to the new side, the crew unclips the end from the old guy and fits it to the mast.*

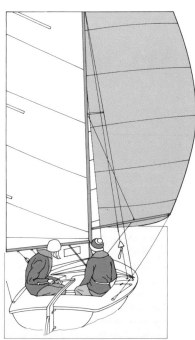

**4** *The crew cleats the new guy and sits down on the windward side, before taking control of the sheet. The helmsman steers on the new course.*

# Playing the spinnaker

Getting a spinnaker to set well demands concentration and skill on the part of the helmsman and crew. The aim is to keep the luff of the sail on the point of curling. To do this, you will have to adjust the sheet constantly, and it should therefore never be cleated. On a reach, when the boat is likely to sail at its fastest, the sheet is often under a lot of strain, and you may find the spinnaker hard to trim. The closer to the wind you sail, the more crucial the sail trim becomes, and the more the helmsman and crew must be alert to the danger of the sail collapsing. It is the helmsman's job to bear away if he thinks a collapse is imminent. However, the spinnaker will not set well unless the crew has

*Below, in strong winds the spinnaker will try to take charge. When the gust hit neither boat was ready to take advantage of it, and so as a consequence, below right, one boat capsized while the other just managed to survive, its spinnaker flogging wildly.*

adjusted the pole height and angle correctly. The clews of the spinnaker should be kept level and the pole should be positioned as far aft as possible without the spinnaker collapsing. If you have difficulty getting the sail to fill, allow the spinnaker pole to be angled further forward, but not so far as to touch the forestay, even when the boat is on a beam reach. In strong winds, especially on a run, the sail will tend to set higher, and you may find it advisable, if the boat starts to roll, to sheet the sail further forward by passing the sheet through the leeward reaching hook rather than through the sheet lead. This will hold the sail down and give it a flatter shape, making it easier to control. In medium strength winds, the spinnaker halyard can be lowered a little, say 15 to 20cm (6 to 8in) to allow the sail to be set further forwards, away from the mainsail. In light winds, if the sail is not filling properly, lower the pole to bring the clews level, and to tension the luff slightly.

# Marking the sheets

One way of making hoisting to windward, chute hoisting and gybing easier is to mark on the spinnaker sheets the points at which they are cleated for correct sail setting. For hoisting to windward, each sheet should be marked at the point at which it passes through the cleat when the clew has just cleared the forestay. This means that the guy can be cleated accurately before hoisting to windward. To find this point, before going afloat, take each clew in turn to a point about 1m (3ft) up the forestay. Cleat the sheet so that it is taut and mark the position on the sheet with paint or coloured twine. To help you set the spinnaker square across the bow before gybing, hoist the spinnaker ashore and trim it so that it sets symmetrically in front of the boat. Cleat both sheets and mark them at the relevant points, using different coloured twine or paint from the hoisting markings. When sailing, once you have set

the sheets to their marked positions, you will only have to make some minor adjustments.
When sailing with a spinnaker hoisted it is important that the crew sits to windward where he is able to see the luff of the sail clearly. This means that on a run or a broad reach, the helmsman must usually sit to leeward to balance the boat. On a beam reach or a close reach, the helmsman sits to leeward as long as the boat can be held upright. The crew should move out on the trapeze as soon as the boat starts to heel, even before the helmsman moves to windward. The helmsman should aim to balance the boat to keep the crew out on the wire in order to give him a better view of the spinnaker luff.

*Right, a spinnaker set well in trying conditions – with the sun behind the spinnaker, the crew has a difficult job to achieve the best possible set.*

# TRAPEZING

Many sailing dinghies these days carry a large area of sail, and if they are to be kept upright and balanced when sailing to windward in moderate to strong winds, the crew will have to shift their weight as far outboard as possible, using a trapeze.

A standard trapeze system (right) suspends the crew on wires which run from the hounds to the side-decks. The crew, wearing a specially designed harness, clips onto a ring on the wire and swings out, his feet on the gunwale and his body supported horizontally by the tapeze wire. Although a trapezing crew looks spectacular, and the sailing is exhilarating, the technique requires only reasonable agility on the part of the crew, together with some practice, as long as the boat is steered by a competent helmsman. In cold climates, the crew must wear a wetsuit and plenty of insulating clothing.

*Right, a standard trapeze system, commonly fitted on most racing boats. Below, a more sophisticated type, known as a continuous trapeze system, allows the crew to move across the boat without having to unhook and clip on again.*

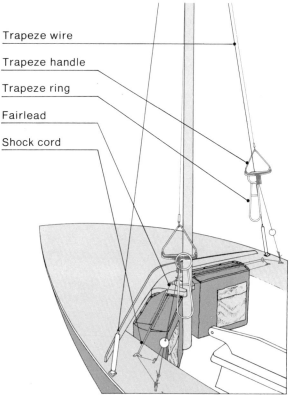

Trapeze wire
Trapeze handle
Trapeze ring
Fairlead
Shock cord

# How to trapeze

If you are a novice at trapezing, you need to have an experienced helmsman steering the boat so that he can compensate for any mistakes you may make. Once the boat starts to heel, the helmsman will tell you to go out on the trapeze. You clip yourself onto the windward ring, and, keeping the jib sheet in the hand nearest the stern, you move onto the side-decking as shown in the sequence below. It looks more precarious than it feels in practice. Once out on the trapeze you should be balanced on the balls of your feet with your legs slightly apart. If the wind strength is insufficient to allow you to fully extend yourself (as in step 5 below), bend your knees slightly to move your weight in towards the boat.

Left, a correctly fitted trapeze harness. The broad back section gives full support to your body, and the hook is fixed to a metal plate at the front. It must fit snugly (the straps are adjustable) so that the hook is just below your waist.

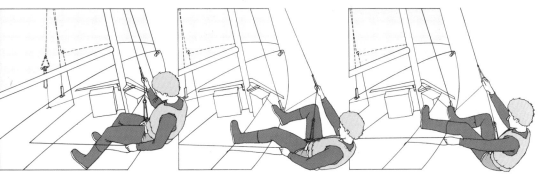

**1** Sitting well out, hook the trapeze ring onto the harness. With your front (bow) hand, grab the handle and pull it outboard.

**2** Slide out over the side-decking and drop down until your weight is on the wire. Twist your body forward, and rest your front (bow) foot on the gunwale by the shroud.

**3** Using the jib sheet to balance, push out with your front (bow) leg against the gunwale, keeping your body at right angles to the boat, if possible.

**4** Bring your back (aft) leg out to rest on the gunwale. Release the handle and continue to straighten your legs.

**5** Lean back with your legs a shoulder's width apart. Hold your front (bow) arm out behind you for more righting power.

# Getting in

You should find that coming in from the trapeze is much simpler than going out. It is a technique you need to practise, as you must be ready to come in rapidly if the wind drops or the helmsman changes direction. If you fail, you are likely to get a ducking! When you come in, make sure that your bow (front) foot doesn't slip forward of the shroud, and try to keep your body at right angles to the boat throughout the manoeuvre. If the boat has not got a continuous trapeze system, unhook yourself from the wire when you come in before a tack.

# Trapezing techniques

As a novice, most of your energy will be taken up by simply getting in and out on the trapeze and trying to keep your body straight once you are out. However, the main job of the trapezing crew is to balance the boat. A good trapezing crew adjusts his or her position constantly to keep the boat sailing upright. If the wind drops or the boat bears away, you can bring your weight more inboard by bending your knees. To get your weight further outboard you can hook onto the lower part of the ring, which will enable you to lie out in a more horizontal position. You can help adjust the fore-and-aft trim of the boat by moving along the gunwale. When the boat is planing you need to be well aft to help the bow rise out of the water. The trapezing crew also has to trim the jib, so don't get so carried away that you forget to watch the set of the sails.

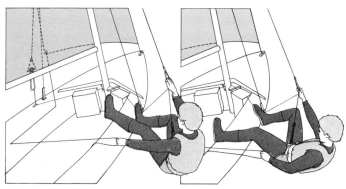

**1** *Lean back slightly, towards the stern of the boat, bend your knees and grasp the handle. Bring your back (stern) leg over the gunwale, taking the strain on your front (bow) leg. Use the jib sheet to steady yourself as you come in towards the boat.*

**2** *Continue to move into the boat taking care not to let your front (bow) leg slip forward of the shroud and keeping your body at right angles to the boat. Once seated on the side-decking, unhook the trapeze ring.*

*Right, to unhook the trapeze ring from your harness, simply knock the ring down so it slips out from underneath the hook of the harness.*

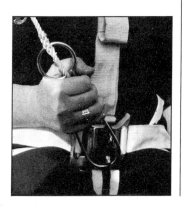

*Above the trapezing crew is standing relatively high and well aft, since the boat is planing. The high position helps the crew to clear the waves.*

The object of the trapezing crew is to exert the maximum righting power while positioning himself to create as little windage as possible, right and below. From the helmsman's point of view, the trapezing crew performs yet another vital role – keeping him dry!

# ROUGH WEATHER TECHNIQUES

It is hard to define rough weather, since conditions that may be safe enough for one type of boat, when sailed by an experienced crew, may be quite beyond the abilities of a less experienced sailor in a different boat. As a general guide any wind strength above Force 5 (20 knots) can be considered as rough weather, although a lot depends on the size of the waves, and the type of waters in which you are sailing. If the wind direction and tidal stream are opposed to each other, the sea will tend to build up, making the conditions a lot more difficult to cope with. A wind strength of even Force 4 (15 knots), coupled with a heavy sea, could present a greater problem than a higher wind strength with calmer water.

Although sailing clubs will usually cancel any organized events and race meetings in strong wind conditions, and may even discourage individuals from sailing, you do need to gain experience of sailing in bad weather, and the best solution is to practice with an experienced helmsman, and to have a rescue boat standing by in case of trouble. The rougher the conditions the better prepared both boat and crew must be. All the fittings and equipment should first be checked to make sure that they are not worn, and that they will be able to take the extra strain of strong winds. The buoyancy and bailing equipment should also be checked.

You can do a lot to help the boat's performance in strong winds by making adjustments to the tuning of the rig. The sail controls can be adjusted so that the sails will spill excess power automatically from the top, by allowing the mast to bend. The flatter the mainsail, the less power it will have. This can be induced by tightening the clew outhaul, the kicking strap and the cunningham control. You should have the widest possible sheeting angle on the jib and mainsail, so that the driving force is directed forwards, lessening the heeling effect.

## Close-hauled

In heavy weather, sailing close-hauled is usually the safest point of sailing, as power can be reduced by spilling wind from the sails (by inducing twist into them or by letting out the sheets). The technique for sailing upwind in strong winds and large waves varies to some extent according to the type of boat you are sailing – whether high-performance dinghy or heavy family one. However, you must always keep the boat as upright as possible, regardless of its type, and both helmsman and crew should use their full righting power by sitting out as far as possible, using the trapeze if there is one. When sailing a modern high-performance boat that will plane to windward, you should sail slightly free of close-hauled until the boat begins to plane, and then you should try to sail as close to the wind as possible while keeping the boat planing. The crew should ease the jib slightly and the helmsman must keep the boat as upright as possible, by playing the mainsheet, which therefore should never be cleated. Both the mainsail and jib should have some twist in them, and you will help reduce the heeling force if you raise the centreboard slightly.

When sailing in large waves, the techniques are much the same for both high-performance and family boats. The helmsman must watch the oncoming waves very carefully and adjust the tiller constantly, to guide the boat over and around the waves so that they don't stop the boat dead in its tracks. If the boat does stall, the driving force and control will be reduced. Boat trim is extremely important: the helmsman and crew should position themselves close together just aft of amidships, so that the bow is able to lift freely over the waves. As a wave approaches the bow, the helmsman should luff up to sail over the face of the wave, and bear away as the boat travels down the back of it. In really large waves, the wind strength increases at the crest of the wave, and both helmsman and crew must move their weight out rapidly to balance the increased heeling force. In a heavy family dinghy, you need to vary the technique a little, as the boat will not normally plane. Your best plan is to use the no go zone to reduce the heeling force, and to help you keep the boat sailing upright. If you use the following technique, you can sail very close to the wind: as a gust approaches luff up a little and let out the mainsheet enough to bring the boat upright. Then, as the gust passes, bear away onto your original course and sheet in. Be careful not to luff up too much, or the boat will slow down and you will lose control. The crew should keep the jib sheeted in hard, unless the wind gusts particularly strongly.

# Reaching

In rough weather, the beam reach, which in moderate or light wind conditions is considered an easy point of sailing, becomes a very fast and difficult course to control. Because of the power created by the strong winds, a high-performance boat is likely to plane continuously. As with upwind sailing, you must be constantly on the look-out for gusts – failure to anticipate and deal with them will result in the end of the boom hitting the water, leading to a capsize. The sails must be adjusted constantly, and the sheets must never be cleated. Just before a gust strikes the boat, the helmsman bears away and the sails are eased. As the gust hits the boat and it accelerates, the sails must be sheeted in again to keep the boat sailing efficiently. The helmsman and crew should sit close together, well aft, to keep the bow lifted. The harder the gusts blow, the further away from the wind the helmsman will have to steer and the further aft he and the crew will have to sit. The centreboard should be just under halfway down to allow the boat to bear away on large waves. When the gust passes, in order to maintain the apparent wind at a constant angle and strength, the helmsman should regain speed by luffing up.

As the boat is sailing parallel to the waves on a reaching course, its progress will not be restricted in the same way as when close-hauled, but do not sail straight down the face of a wave, or the bow will dig into the one in front. Bear away down the face of the waves at a slight angle and, as the boat accelerates, luff up a little to travel on the same wave for as long as possible. However, be careful not to stay on a wave so long that you end up to leeward of your objective. The crew weight should be forward as the bow moves down the waves, and should then move aft as the boat accelerates.

*Below, sailing in strong winds is exciting but you must be able to handle the boat at high speed and in waves. When planing, keep the boat upright and move your weight aft to lift the bow.*

*Any high-performance dinghy like the 470, above, will plane easily on reaching courses in strong winds.*

# Running

In rough weather, the run is the least attractive course to sail. It is difficult to balance the boat as there is no heeling force. On a dead run, the pressure of the wind in the mainsail can cause the top of it to twist forwards of the mast and this will tend to create a violent rocking movement. The best way to combat this is to tighten the kicking strap and, if necessary, sheet in the mainsail slightly as well. Spreading the crew weight on opposite sides of the boat and lowering the centreboard to the halfway-down position (or slightly further down in a single-hander) also helps to reduce rolling. In a two-man boat you can lessen the rolling movement by poling out the jib so that it goosewings. In a single-handed boat the effective area of the mainsail and the turning movement can be reduced by sheeting in the sails until the tell-tales fly out in the opposite direction, indicating that the airflow across the sail has been reversed. This provides a heeling force to leeward which makes the task of balancing the boat much easier.

On a run in rough weather you will find that the waves coming from behind will pick up the boat so that it starts to surf. Unless you take action the boat may begin to overtake the wave in front and bury its bow in the back of it. If this is allowed to happen the boat will slow down dramatically, and the pressure on the rig will increase. This makes the boat unstable and difficult to control. The problem can be avoided if you sail a faster course by luffing onto a broad reach. This enables the boat to traverse the waves as described previously and it will sail faster. The apparent wind will shift ahead and this will also increase the boat speed.

An alternative to sailing on a run, which is often faster for high-performance boats, is to tack downwind, sailing a zig-zag course across the wind by gybing at intervals.

# Tacking and gybing

Changing course through the wind in rough weather demands much greater concentration than in normal conditions, as the increased strength of the wind makes the movements much more violent. Maintaining the balance of the boat is crucial and you must not allow the boat to heel during a tack, or during a gybe or you are likely to capsize.

When tacking in rough weather the most important factor is maintaining the speed of the boat during the turn. It must be moving fast immediately prior to the tack. It is preferable to tack where the waves are smallest and the helmsman must watch carefully to pick the most advantageous moment. Start to tack when the bow has just passed the top of a wave, which reduces the possibility of the boat being stopped by a wave during the tack. The crew releases the jib just as the boat starts to turn and sheets it in as soon as possible on the new side. The helmsman and crew must sit well out on the new windward side as quickly as they can, to prevent the boat heeling. Do not sheet in the sails tightly until the boat has picked up speed again.

Gybing in strong winds and large waves is a critical manoeuvre which must be tackled smoothly and precisely. The best moment to gybe is when the boat is moving at its fastest, either down a wave or after accelerating from a gust. At this point the apparent wind is at its weakest and therefore the pressure on the rig is least, so the boom moves across the boat more easily. It is very important when gybing the boat that the boom is not allowed to touch the shroud or it may break or snap the mast or the shroud during a gybe.

*Left, sailing in rough weather requires balance and feel, but particularly so on downwind courses when the boat may roll a great deal in waves.*

*Right, in heavy weather you must keep the boat moving fast, and upright, before tacking.*

# RACING

Most people, once they have acquired a reasonable amount of skill, are keen to pit their skills against other sailors. As a novice, the best solution is to crew for an experienced helmsman in your first few races, before taking the helm yourself. Some people, of course, specialize in crewing and have no desire to be at the helm anyway. Racing a dinghy in properly organized events provides an excellent incentive to improve your sailing techniques.

At local level, dinghy racing is normally organized through sailing clubs. At a wider level, it is often organized by the class associations for the different types of boat. So, if you want to race, join a club if you haven't already done so. If you already own a boat, you must, of course, find a club that will accept your boat, and which provides racing for that class of boat. If you are not a boat-owner yet, but plan to be, then join a club which provides the type of sailing you want to indulge in, and also accepts the class of boat you want to buy.

There are a number of ways in which the races can be organized; usually they will be set according to the design or class of boat, or by the use of a handicap system. The courses will also vary but they are laid out to test the sailor's skill on different points of sailing and will normally be set around three or four marker buoys, with different legs on successive laps.

As a novice sailor, unless you happen to be crewing for an excellent helmsman, you are unlikely to win your first races. You can, however, concentrate on improving your own position relative to other sailors with roughly the same skills. One of the best ways of improving your own performance is to watch the leaders carefully, noting their rig adjustments and the way they are sailing their boats.

Although it is beyond most beginners to master all the rules, they must be familiar with the most important ones (see pages 138–40). A rule handbook should be studied, and practice will help you to acquire a better understanding of the more esoteric rules.

If you intend to race your own boat, it will have to be measured and given a certificate by your class association (unless it is a second-hand boat and already possesses a valid certificate). The rules of different class associations vary. Whereas some boats are strict one-designs, others are restricted development boats. In the former category, there can be little or no deviation from the basic design; in the latter, the boat has only to conform to broad rules on hull length and rig. Even in the former class there are small differences, known as tolerances, and some variations are allowed in the fittings. However, if you win a one-design race you can be assured that it is your sailing skill which is responsible.

*Above, a fleet of Optimists round a leeward mark in perfect conditions.*

*Right, 505s struggling with a spinnaker gybe on a fairly gusty day.*

# Racing courses

Since sailing clubs, at local level, set their own courses, you will find a marked difference in the way courses are set up. The race organizers will normally try to test the competitors' skills as much as possible, and they will usually ensure that some marks are rounded to port and others to starboard, and that the markers are so arranged as to introduce as many points of sailing as possible. To a large extent, however, the course set will be limited by the type of waters and the wind conditions. Some clubs may use their own markers for the race, others – particularly on tidal waters – may use permanent ones such as navigation marks. The course to be sailed will be indicated on a board before the start of each race, and you must note it carefully. Failure to follow the correct course will result in automatic disqualification. Starting lines and starting procedure are perhaps the most complex single aspect of racing (see pages 136–7).

*Lark dinghies rounding a windwark mark in a Championship race in light airs.*

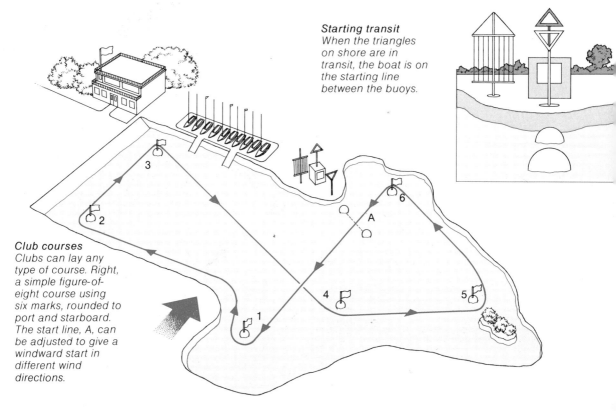

***Starting transit***
*When the triangles on shore are in transit, the boat is on the starting line between the buoys.*

***Club courses***
*Clubs can lay any type of course. Right, a simple figure-of-eight course using six marks, rounded to port and starboard. The start line, A, can be adjusted to give a windward start in different wind directions.*

# Open meetings

Clubs holding open meetings will normally use the basic championship course, below, but without the third leg, so that the course consists of a simple triangular one with the starting line laid square to the wind (using a committee boat). Three markers are usually laid in an equilateral triangle with two of the markers to windward and leeward, and the third between the other two. Normally the first lap incorporates a beat and two reaches, the second lap would be around the windward and leeward buoys alone to give a beat and a run, and the final leg would be a beat up to the finish line. On these courses, the buoys are left to port and the start is at the leeward mark and the finish at the windward mark.

# Championship course

The course used for a championship event is usually based on the Olympic course below. The start and finish lines are usually to leeward of the leeward mark and to windward of the windward mark to give a slightly longer first and last beat. Normally four laps are sailed, a triangle for the first lap, a beat and run for the second, a further triangle for the third, and a final beat up to the finishing line. Most championship events are held on the sea, and the courses laid well away from the land to ensure as steady conditions as possible.

**Key**
- ● Mark
- ○ Mark disregarded
- ●┄┄▐ Starting or finishing line

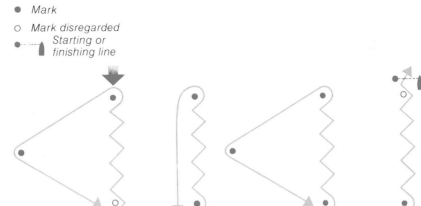

The first lap has a beat and two broad reaches.

The second lap has a beat and a run.

The third lap has a beat and two broad reaches.

The last lap has a beat up to the finishing line.

# Alternative course

Critics of the Olympic course say that it places a premium on beating, broad reaching and running and fails to incorporate a beam reach. An alternative course, right, has been designed to test crews on more points of sailing and is under consideration by the racing authorities.

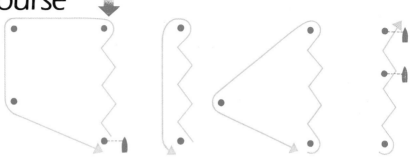

The first lap has a beat, a beam reach, a run and a broad reach.

The second lap has a beat and a run.

The third lap has a beat and two broad reaches.

The last lap has a beat with a choice of finishing lines.

# Types of race

Although boat-for-boat racing in one-design classes and restricted development classes provides exciting competition, there are other forms of racing you may come across. Most clubs organize handicap events, in which boats of different classes can race against each other, and it is a popular form with race committees who want as many boats competing as possible. Team racing is popular in colleges and universities, and in some clubs, where it is the overall team score which counts, not the individual competitor. This involves a greater understanding of tactics, and has less emphasis on faster sailing. Finally, and more unusually nowadays, there is match racing where only two boats compete against each other. The most famous event of this type, although for 12-metre keeled boats rather than dinghies, is the America's Cup, which is raced triennially.

Team racing is normally organized between two teams of three or four boats, all in the same class. A match usually consists of two races, with the teams exchanging boats in between races. The object is for the team, rather than any individual boat, to win. The scoring system is organized in such a way that a team with second, third and fourth places, for example, can beat a team with first, fifth and sixth places. Thus the emphasis is less on individual prowess and boat speed and more on tactical ability. A good knowledge of the rules is vital, as is the ability to evaluate the overall team position and act accordingly. For instance, if you are in third place with your team members in fourth and fifth places, you will lose unless you can find a way of slowing down the opposition's boat in second position, so that your own team members can pass him. Team racing is undoubtedly one of the best ways to improve both your boat handling skills and your knowledge of the racing rules.

Handicap racing is commonly used in clubs where no one class of boats in the club has enough members to make single class racing worthwhile. However, it is also commonly used in clubs where there are enough boats for some single class races, but where there is also a wide variety of types of boat. The most widely used handicapping system is based on "yardstick" numbers which are given to each class of dinghy. When a mixed fleet of dinghies race against each other, the time each boat takes to complete the course is recorded and a corrected time in relation to the appropriate yardstick number is worked out to give the finishing positions. The yardstick numbers are modified as evidence is gathered from different clubs, in an effort to make the system as fair as possible. In addition to handicapping the classes of boat, some clubs handicap individual helmsmen. At the start of each season a helmsman with a proven consistent record is given a "scratch" rating. Other helmsman are then awarded handicaps around this level on the basis of their known ability, and the handicaps are adjusted after each race result.

The classic form of racing between two boats of the same class, match racing, is often conducted in the form of a series of races between pairs of competitors making up a tournament. Each competitor must race against every other competitor in the series and the overall winner is the one with most wins. The match is often won or lost at the start line, since the boat which gets off ahead can control the boat behind to some extent.

*Class racing in popular one designs like these Enterprises is a good test of helmsmanship as there is little variation in boat performance.*

*In handicap races, like the one left, you should avoid involvement with other boats wherever possible, as you are competing against the clock rather than against other boats.*

# Preparing for a race

Getting your boat ready for a race may take some time, particularly if it has a fairly complex rig. It is important to make sure that the rig is properly adjusted for the conditions, and that all the equipment is in sound working order. See that the outside of the hull is smooth and clean – a dirty hull will affect your boat speed. If any of the rigging or equipment is worn, replace it before it fails. You will be furious if you lose a race because a shroud snaps or a halyard breaks.

If your class rules or the race instructions demand that you carry certain items of equipment, make sure they are stowed securely on board. These might include an anchor and warp, or a paddle, for example. Make sure you carry a protest flag (see page 139).

You should wear the right clothes for the conditions, and you should wear clothing that will not only keep you warm, but will not restrict your movement or create wind resistance. If the race is likely to be a long one, make sure you have a supply of food and drink with you – while you may not have time to eat during the race, a glucose enriched drink, for example, will give you some extra energy.

Before launching, read through the sailing instructions for the race and familiarize yourself with the course to be sailed and the scoring system in operation. If you are unclear or confused on any points, talk to the race officers before you go out. Take the instructions with you in a sealed plastic folder, so that you can refer to them if necessary. If the racing rules stipulate that you must have a safety disc or tally with you, make sure you don't forget it. Failure to carry one, if stipulated, could lead to disqualification. This can also apply if the competitor fails to return the disc within a certain time limit after the race has ended.

## Scoring systems

Many racing events are organized as a series of races in which the winner is the boat that achieves the best overall score. There are various scoring systems used, and you should make sure you understand which one is in operation, and how it is organized, so that you can assess your position relative to that of your rivals as the series continues. Most major events use the Olympic scoring system. In this, there are ideally seven races but at least no fewer than five. The winning boat has the least number of points and they are allocated as follows: zero for first place, 3 points for second place, 5.7 for third place, 8 points for fourth place, 10 for fifth, and 11.7 for sixth; for all placings lower down, you will be allocated the place position plus 6 points so that if you were tenth for example, you would score 16 points. Any boats which fail to start, or retire, or are disqualified, are allocated points equal to the number of entrants in the race plus one point. However, one result can be discarded by each competitor and the one with the lowest overall score for the remaining results is the winner.

# Starting lines

The simplest form of starting line is that using an onshore transit (see page 132), at least from the point of view of the organizers. Most races are set with the start on a windward leg, and, of course, there are limitations to the ways in which a starting line using an onshore transit can be moved to take account of wind changes. In this case, a committee boat (see page 138) is generally used. Where there is a large fleet competing, a gate start (opposite) is sometimes used instead, as it saves congestion on the starting line, although opponents argue that it increases it at the first mark.

*Below, a windward start for a fleet of Fireballs using a simple committee boat start line.*

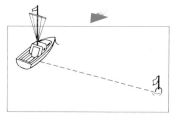

**Simple committee boat start line**
*With a committee boat start line, it is easier to ensure that the start is to windward. It does, however, require a suitable committee boat and race organizers with the knowledge to lay good starting lines. The line itself is usually between the mast of the committee boat and an outer mark.*

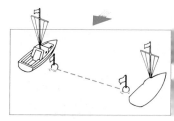

**Committee boat start with two buoys**
*Similar to the start, left, but with the addition of an inner limit mark to keep competitors away from the committee boat. The committee boat can be at either end of the start line and doesn't have to anchor. As a result the line angle can be shifted easily if the wind changes.*

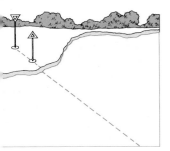

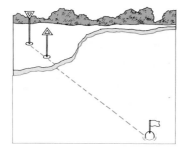

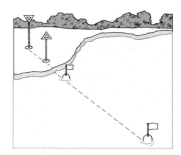

**Onshore transit with no outer or inner limit mark**
This is the simplest form of start line using a transit onshore to define a line. However, the amount that the transit can be moved to take account of changes in wind direction to provide a windward start is often limited.

**Onshore transit with outer limit mark**
This line is similar to the first, but uses an outer limit mark beyond which competitors may not start. The mark does not have to be on the line which is defined solely by the transits, but it helps the competitor if it is.

**Onshore transit with inner and outer limit marks**
This type of line has marks at each end to define the area in which boats must start. The marks need not be on the transit line, but it is best if they are.

# Gate start

With this type of start, which has to be set on a windward leg, the starting line is defined by a boat, already designated as the pathfinder before the start of the race, sailing away from a committee boat. About 30 seconds before the start of the race, the pathfinder sails away from the committee boat, close-hauled on a port tack, followed by the gate launch. A third boat, the guard boat, is positioned to leeward of the pathfinder to prevent it being fouled by other boats. Approximately 10 seconds before the start, the gate launch drops a free-floating marker buoy to indicate the inner limit of the line. As soon as the start is signalled the competitors can cross the line formed between the mark and the stern of the gate launch. The pathfinder continues

on port tack until signalled to join the race by the gate launch, which then drops another marker buoy to indicate the outer limit of the starting line. Participating boats in a gate start must be careful not to be to windward of the pathfinder, or they will get caught on the wrong side of the line and may be unable to return. Approach the stern of the guard boat close-hauled on a starboard tack, not on a reach, so that you can't get trapped between a close-hauled boat and the guard boat. If you collided in this position, you would be disqualified.

After dropping the inner limit mark, the gate launch closely follows the pathfinder with the guard boat to leeward. The boats which have crossed the path of the gate launch have started, while the others are still waiting.

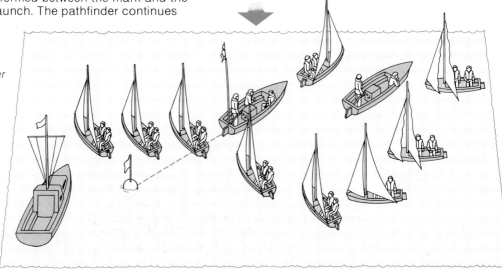

# Flags and signals

At most race meetings, instructions and information about the racing is conveyed on the water by sound signals of various types, and by the use of flags. The normal systems use the international code flags, but the racing rules give the flags meanings that differ from their normal ones.

The flags, right, are those you are most likely to encounter in the course of a meeting. Always check with the race instructions to make sure what system is being used. Any flags used are generally displayed on either the committee boat or the starting box. Often several flags will be displayed simultaneously, and when they are each hoisted, or broken out, attention is drawn to them by one or more sound signals.

The actual timing of the start is always governed by the visual signals, not the sound signals. It helps to have a card aboard the boat giving the flag shapes and colours, as well as a copy of the sailing instructions. Both should be stowed in a dry place.

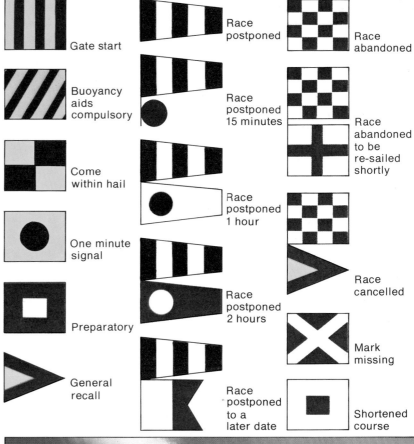

Gate start

Buoyancy aids compulsory

Come within hail

One minute signal

Preparatory

General recall

Race postponed

Race postponed 15 minutes

Race postponed 1 hour

Race postponed 2 hours

Race postponed to a later date

Race abandoned

Race abandoned to be re-sailed shortly

Race cancelled

Mark missing

Shortened course

*Right, a committee boat at the start line. The preparatory flag indicates that there is less than five minutes before the start.*

# Rules

You must have a clear idea of the rules when you race. To start with, familiarity with the basic rules will be enough. But as your racing skills develop, and tactics play a greater part in your racing, you will need to know something of the finer points. The rules are set out in the official rule book of the International Yacht Racing Union (IYRU), available through your national sailing authority. They are also available in the form of explanatory books. Some of the most basic rules are given here and overleaf. If you are inexperienced, and in any doubts about your rights, keep clear!

*Clear astern – definition*
*A boat is clear astern of another when it is behind an imaginary line drawn at right angles from the aftermost part of the hull of the other – red is clear astern of green (above) and overlaps yellow.*

*Opposite tack*
*A boat on port tack (red) must keep clear of a boat on starboard tack (green). (Rule 36)*

*Same tack – overlapped*
*When overlapped, a windward boat (red) must keep clear of a leeward boat (green). (Rule 37)*

*Same tack – clear astern*
*A boat clear astern (red) must keep clear of a boat clear ahead (green). (Rule 37)*

*Same tack – luffing*
*After the start, a boat clear ahead or to leeward may luff at will. Thus the green boat may luff and the red boat must keep clear. A restriction is described right. (Rule 38)*

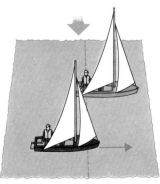

*Sighting abeam*
*If the helmsman of the windward (green) boat, when looking across his boat, can see that he is ahead of the mast of the leeward (red) boat, the latter may not luff.*

# Protests

If you get involved in an incident, and know that you are in the wrong, you should comply with the penalty set out in the sailing instructions. However, if you think that another boat is at fault, not you, then you must show the protest flag below, attached to a shroud, and inform the race officer as soon as possible after the race.

# Marks and obstructions

If there is likely to be any infringement of the rules when racing, it is almost certain to occur when boats are jostling for position round a mark. You must be aware of your rights if you are to gain the best position while avoiding collision – other boats are quite likely to demand room when they are not entitled to it. Careful study of the rule book on these points is necessary. The situations below are ones that commonly occur. Always be prepared to respond quickly if a boat with right of way hails for more room, and take care not to get yourself into an awkward situation. Any boat which touches a mark will normally have to go back and round it again, although in some cases it may have to retire.

*Stars in trouble rounding a windward mark. The boat in the foreground is in irons, blocking the way for the boats approaching from behind. Several boats are on port tack, and have no right of way over those on starboard tack.*

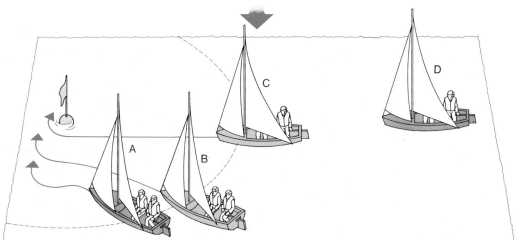

### Above, rounding marks
*When two or more boats are about to round or pass a mark or obstruction on the same side, an outside boat must give room to any boat overlapping it on the inside. A gives way to B and C, but B gives way only to C. Boats clear astern may only establish an inside overlap when the boat ahead is more than two boat lengths from the mark or obstruction. Therefore D may not ask A, B or C for room. (Rule 42)*

### Right, hailing for room at obstructions
*This rule applies when two close-hauled boats are approaching an obstruction on the same tack. If the boat which is to leeward or ahead (A) has to tack, it may hail the other boat (B) for room. (Rule 43)*

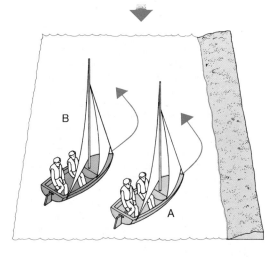

*Opposite, three Gull dinghies bearing away around a wing mark. The leader is clear ahead but 1939 may have to give way to 2202, if the latter has an overlap.*

# TUNING A BOAT

To get the best possible performance out of your boat you have to learn how to tune the rig so that it can be adjusted to suit different sailing conditions. In light to moderate winds you should be looking for ways of increasing the driving force of the sails while reducing any drag caused by the hull and the standing rigging. In stronger breezes, you will be looking for ways of keeping a reasonable amount of driving power in the sails, while trying to reduce the heeling force of the boat.

In the old days boats would have more than one suit of sails, each suit cut to suit different wind conditions. Although some racing boats still do so today, most modern boats have a number of controls on the boat which enable you to adjust the shape of the sails for the different conditions.

Getting the best out of the rig is largely a matter of experience, trying out the boat in different wind strengths and with various adjustments made to see how it sails. There are, however, certain general rules which can be applied and you should know how to use the various sail shape controls.

As a guide, most boats sail in moderate breezes with the designed fullness of the sail. In higher wind strengths (and in very light breezes when you wish to maintain the airflow without disturbance) you should try to flatten the sails. To reduce the heeling power in strong winds, it helps if you can increase the gap between the jib leech and the mainsail luff (known as the jib slot) and also if you induce twist into the top of the sails to allow them to spill wind.

The controls you use to produce these effects will vary from boat to boat, but usually you will need to adjust the fore-and-aft and lateral bend of the mast (by changing the position of the spreaders and the tension on the shrouds and forestay). For the mainsail alone, you can adjust the cunningham control, clew outhaul, kicking strap, mainsheet tension, traveller position and battens; and for the jib alone, you can adjust the jib halyard and fairleads, and sheet tension.

The position of the jib in relation to the mainsail is of critical importance to the set of the sails. The jib usually overlaps the mainsail to some extent and the gap between the jib leech and the mainsail luff is known as the jib slot. This slot can be narrowed (up to a point) to increase driving power and widened to reduce it. It is important the slot is parallel all the way up. The position of maximum curve in the sails is always of great importance in getting the boat to sail well, and most of the controls act on this curve in some way. In general, the maximum curve should be about halfway between the luff and leech in the mainsail, and slightly further forward in the headsail.

Initially you can adjust the rig ashore, putting the boat on its trolley in a light breeze and turning it, fully rigged into the close-hauled position. Tension the controls as necessary to get the point of maximum draught in the right place, and make sure that there are no creases (vertical or horizontal) in either of the sails. Adjust the mainsheet to position the boom down the centreline of the boat, and then adjust the jib fairlead and sheet tension to get the slot parallel. The final tuning can be done afloat.

*The slot between the mainsail and jib should be parallel all the way up.*

# Masts

One of the major factors affecting sail shape is the amount the mast can be induced to bend. Masts are usually of wood or aluminium alloy – the latter is more commonly used today, since it is not affected by changes in humidity and therefore gives consistent bending. Although the mast itself cannot be adjusted, the fittings attached to it can be used to alter the angle of mast rake, and fore-and-aft or lateral bend. In light to moderate sailing conditions, the mast is kept fairly straight, giving the sail its designed fullness. To flatten the mainsail in stronger winds, the mast is induced to bend fore-and-aft and to leeward at its top, which gives twist to the sail, reducing pressure at the top. By allowing the mast to bend as the wind increases, you not only produce a flattened and twisted mainsail, but you widen the slot between the jib leech and the mainsail luff, which also helps to reduce the driving force of the sails.

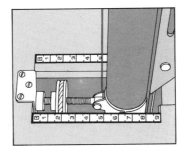

**Mast bend fore and aft**
*Sail becomes flatter.*

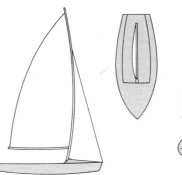

**Sideways bend**
*Mast straight (left) and bent to leeward (right).*

**Mast ram**
*This device controls the amount the mast can move forward at deck level, giving additional control over fore-and-aft mast bend low down.*

---

# Spreaders and shrouds

The spreaders are one of the principal means of creating or controlling mast bend. They join the mid-section of the mast to the shrouds, and the amount by which they distort the shrouds from their natural straight line determines the behaviour of the mast under sail. You must realize that only the windward shroud and spreader are under strain when the boat is sailing, and hence are the only ones which affect mast bend. The length of the spreaders and the setting angle can be altered to produce different forms of mast bend. If the spreaders are angled aft, they will pull the shroud aft with them, with the result that the centre of the mast is pushed forwards and the top part bends aft. If the spreaders are angled forwards, the opposite effect is achieved and fore-and-aft mast bend is reduced. If the spreaders are short, known as being in tension, they will induce sideways mast bend, pulling the middle of the mast to windward, and if they are long, pushing the shrouds out of their natural line, they will reduce lateral bend. The effect of the spreaders on the mast can be altered by varying the tension in the shrouds and the jib luff. The tension is normally adjusted by altering the jib halyard tension or by using shroud tension adjusters. Highly tensioned rigging will increase the effect of the spreaders, and loosely tensioned rigging will reduce it.

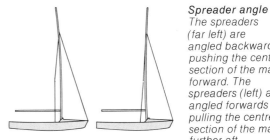

**Spreader angle**
*The spreaders (far left) are angled backwards, pushing the centre section of the mast forward. The spreaders (left) are angled forwards pulling the centre section of the mast further aft.*

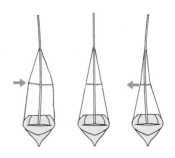

**Spreader length**
*Spreaders in compression (far left), neutral (centre left) and in tension (left).*

# Mainsheet systems

If your boat has a centre mainsheet system with an athwartships traveller, you can use the mainsheet when sailing upwind to adjust the tension on the leech of the sail and to control twist. You can then use the traveller to control the angle of the sail to the centreline of the boat. You will find that by moving the position of the blocks on the boom you can adjust the amount of mast bend. If the blocks are positioned midway along the boom, the pull on the mainsheet is vertical, causing the top of the mast to bend aft. If the blocks are moved aft along the boom, the pull exerts pressure along the boom, which in turn pushes the mast forward near the base inducing forward bend of the mast lower down.

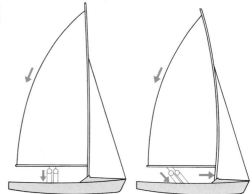

*Far left, with the tension on the mainsheet vertical only the top of the mast is bent but when the mainsheet blocks are moved aft, the tension pushes the middle of the mast forward.*

*A centre mainsheet with an athwartships traveller, used to control the boom angle*

*A centre mainsheet with a raised bar: the mainsheet alone controls the boom angle.*

# Battens

Many people fail to consider the battens when adjusting the rig, because they don't realize that they help control sail shape. All battens should be flexible, regardless of the type, although the degree of flexibility will depend on the design of the sail. A full light-weather sail needs more-flexible battens than a heavy-weather sail, for example. Battens which are not full-length should be tapered in thickness towards the inner ends, to prevent a hard spot forming in the sail. Full-length battens, however, should not be tapered and can be tied in tightly or lightly to increase or reduce the curve of the sail. Each set of battens should be matched to the curve of the sail, and each batten should be marked to show which pocket it fits into.

# Clew outhaul

The clew outhaul – the line stretching from the clew of the sail to the end of the boom – can be used to apply tension to the foot of the mainsail. If it consists of a simple lashing, you cannot adjust it once afloat, but high-performance dinghies usually have an adjustable control with a purchase system inside the boom, and with a line emerging near the mast, and led aft. Applying tension to it will flatten the sail and move the point of maximum draught further aft. To get the designed shape to the sail, pull the clew outhaul just taut enough to get rid of any small vertical creases, but not so tight as to start forming horizontal ones.

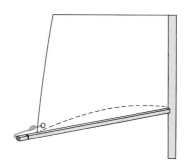

*With the clew outhaul fairly slack, the sail is full.*

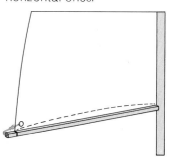

*With the clew outhaul tensioned, the sail is flattened.*

# Cunningham control

The cunningham control is used to apply tension to the luff of the sail. It consists of a line led through the cunningham hole, or to a block attached to it, and secured around the gooseneck. The other end is controlled by a purchase system led back to the helmsman. Normally the tension on the cunningham control should be just sufficient to remove any small horizontal creases in the luff. By increasing the tension you will move the point of maximum draught further forwards, and by reducing it you will move it further aft.

# Kicking strap

The kicking strap helps to prevent the boom from rising and, by keeping the sail leech under tension, helps to control any twist in the sail. When tensioned, it will also induce a certain amount of mast bend, as when the centre mainsheet blocks are set aft. The kicking strap is a useful sail-adjusting control when you are sailing, permitting greater control over the sail shape and thus helping the sail develop power, especially offwind.

*A powerful kicking strap of the lever type, above, can be adjusted from either side of the boat using a double-ended control line.*

# Jib halyard

The jib should be tensioned sufficiently so that the luff of the sail does not sag, and to do this you need a jib halyard which is made of wire. A sagging jib luff will prevent the boat pointing properly to windward and will increase the heeling force of the sail, and it will also alter the shape of the jib slot, as the curve in the sail will move aft making the leech area too full and tight.

# Jib fairleads

The jib fairlead position is of vital importance on windward courses as the fairlead position and the jib sheet tension control the jib leech tension and therefore the slot width, which should be parallel all the way up. Ideally you should have fairleads which can be adjusted both fore-and-aft and laterally so that you can narrow or widen the sheeting angle at will — moving it outboard in rough weather, and inboard in much lighter winds.

# Combining controls

The use of all the various controls affects the sail shape; practice and experience alone will enable you to achieve exactly the effects you desire. If you keep the mast straight, reduce the tension on the mainsheet and the kicking strap, keep the mast ram on, and tension the clew outhaul just enough to pull the foot of the sail to remove any vertical creases, while leaving the cunningham control off, you will end up with a sail with the maximum possible fullness. If, on the other hand, you increase the mast bend by leaving off the ram, and putting a lot of tension on the mainsheet and kicking strap, pulling out the clew outhaul as far as possible, and putting as much tension as possible on the cunningham control, you will end up with a very flat sail. By moving the jib fairlead aft and outwards, you can induce the maximum width of jib slot, thereby reducing the

heeling effect of the sails and increasing power. By moving the jib fairlead forwards and inboard you can narrow the slot to give better pointing ability and more power in lighter winds. These adjustments represent the extremes, and most of your tuning will be aimed at more minor adjustments when afloat. In general, the overall aim should be to develop as much driving force as possible while keeping a balanced boat and helm, and good pointing ability.

*Above left, keeping the mast straight with little tension on any control gives a full sail shape.*

*Above, allowing the mast to bend and tensioning the controls results in the sail becoming very much flatter.*

# KNOTS AND ROPEWORK

Rope forms a vital part of the boat's equipment and is expensive to replace. Learning how to handle rope and to look after it properly are an essential part of your seamanship skills. You will lengthen the life of your ropes if you do not allow them to chafe against sharp or abrasive objects. If they do wear in one place you can sometimes repair them by cutting out the frayed part and splicing the ends together (see page 151). Rope ends should be whipped to prevent them unravelling (see also page 151).

Over the years sailors have added to their repertoire of knots. The selection on these pages includes the most commonly used. Some are multi-purpose knots, others have a more specific task – the rolling hitch, for example, will take strain in one specific direction. Make sure you can tie them quickly and accurately – your safety may well depend on them one day.

# Types of rope

Although rope was formerly made of natural fibres, synthetics are now more commonly used. They are more hard-wearing than natural fibre, but some tend to become slippery when wet.
The actual construction of the rope is either laid – where the strands are twisted together – or braided, where they are interwoven. Mooring warps are usually of three-strand laid construction, while sheets and halyards are usually braided.
The type and thickness of the rope depends largely on its function. Although braided ropes are more durable and more pleasant to handle than the laid variety, they cannot be repaired by splicing.

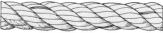
Polypropylene three-strand

Nylon octoplait

Nylon eightplait

Polyester three-strand

Nylon braidline

# Parts of the knot

Knotting, like sailing, has its own terminology. The bend you make in a rope when knotting it is known as the bight. The part of the rope under strain is known as the standing part.

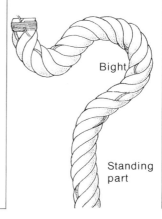

Bight

Standing part

# Figure of eight

The main purpose of this knot is to put a stopper at the end of a rope. It is easy to tie and equally easy to undo.

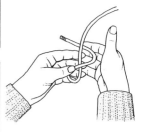

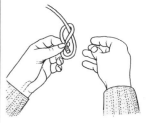

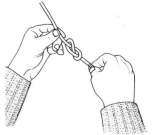

# Reef knot

This knot, originally devised to tie the reefing lines of a sail, is formed from two half-hitches, tied in opposite directions. If you inadvertently tie them in the same direction, the resulting knot will jam. It is known as a "granny knot". Take care to tie the knot exactly as shown.

# Sheet bend

Use this knot to join two ropes of unequal thickness. To undo the knot, bend it in the centre and push the bight down on the half-hitch.

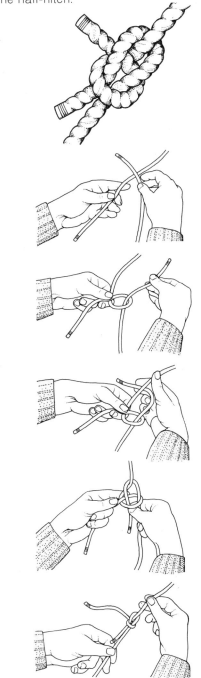

## Undoing a reef knot

A reef knot can be quickly and easily untied by grasping one end of the rope in one hand and the standing part in the other and pushing the knot off the standing part, as shown.

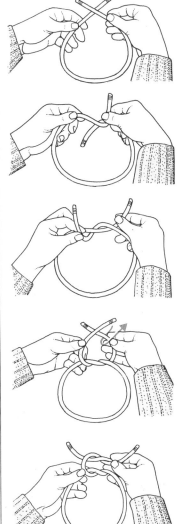

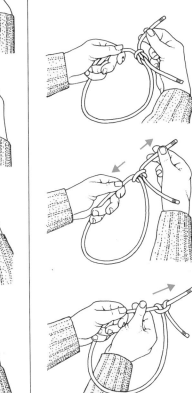

# Round turn and two half-hitches

This is one of the most commonly used knots of all. It is used to tie a rope to any standing object and is easy and quick both to tie and to undo, provided there is no great strain on the rope. Two half-hitches should be sufficient to secure the rope.

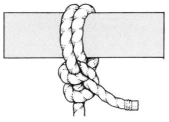

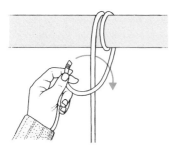

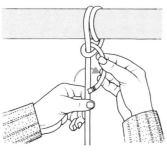

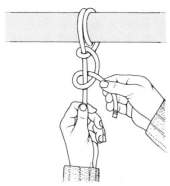

# Clove hitch

Use this knot to tie small items temporarily, such as fenders, to stanchions. It holds well only when under steady strain at right angles to the standing object to which it is fixed. If there is any lateral or jerking strain, it may well come undone.

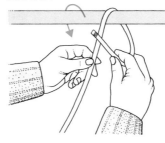

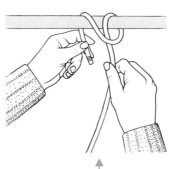

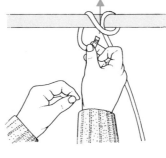

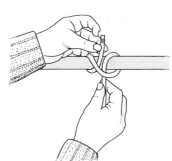

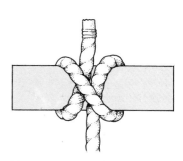

**Clove hitch around a bollard**
If you are tying up temporarily to a bollard, you can use the quick method below. The rope is coiled in the hand, as shown, and the loops dropped over the bollard. Use a half-hitch if you wish to secure the knot more firmly.

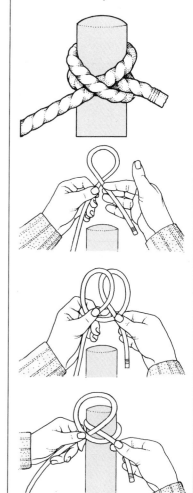

# Bowline

This knot is used for a number of tasks. Since beginners can find it hard to tie, an easy method is shown below – there are others. Learn to tie the knot with the standing part both towards you and away from you.

# Rolling hitch

This knot is useful if you wish to put strain on the knot which is parallel to the object to which it is tied – the more pressure you apply the tighter the knot becomes.

# Becket hitch

This is a useful knot for securing a rope to an eye or hook. Up to step 3 it is known as a single becket hitch. Step 4 turns it into a double becket hitch, which permits the knot to take greater strain.

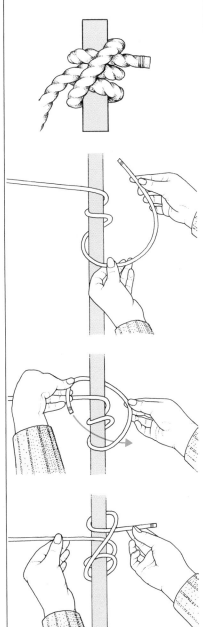

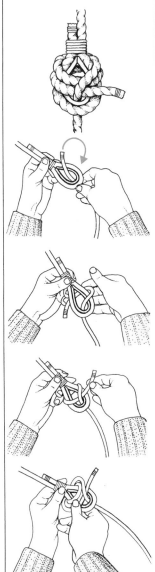

# Quick-release knot

There are a number of knots which can be tied so that they can be released quickly, usually by looping over the end of the rope to tie the knot. The most commonly used is the quick-release version of the round turn and two half-hitches. You can add a further half-hitch (bottom) for a more secure knot, although it will not release quite as quickly.

# Fisherman's bend

This is the recommended knot for attaching a rope to an anchor. It is similar to the round turn and two half-hitches.

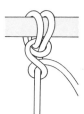

**1** *Make a round turn in the usual way.*

**2** *Double the rope end to form a loop and lay the loop over the standing part.*

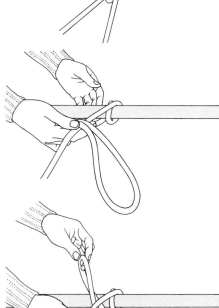

**3** *Make a half-hitch with the loop around the standing part, and pull tight.*

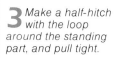

**4** *At this stage, the knot can be quickly released, even under strain, by pulling on the end of the rope.*

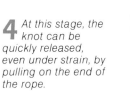

*For greater security, a half-hitch can be made although the knot cannot be released so easily.*

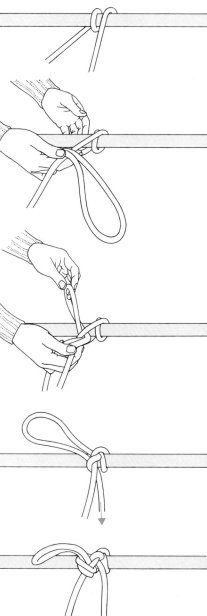

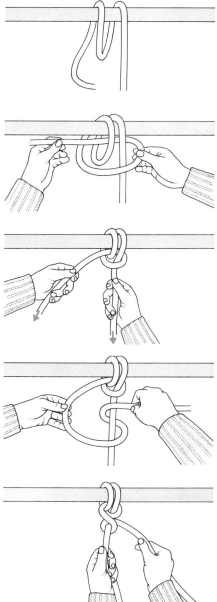

# Whipping

To prevent ropes unravelling, they should be finished by whipping the ends with twine. Be careful to whip in the opposite direction from the lay of the rope.

Finished whipping

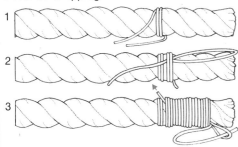

# Splicing

Splicing is a way of joining two ropes by weaving the ends together. You will need a marline spike to separate the strands, and whipping twine to bind the ends while you work.

Finished splice

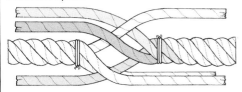

**1** Bind each rope 15cm (6in) away from the end and unravel them to this point. Place the two ends together as shown.

**2** Bind the loose strands of one rope to the other and remove the twine from the first rope. Start to weave in the loose strands in turn as shown above, turning the rope as you work. Continue until each strand has been threaded through at least three times. Repeat the process with the other rope and trim the ends.

# Eye splice

An eye splice is used to form a fixed loop of any size in the end of a rope. It is sometimes put into the end of a mooring warp, and has the advantage of being stronger than any knot.
To make the splice, you must first unlay the strands of the rope for a sufficient distance to complete five full tucks under the strands. Whip the rope to prevent the strands unravelling before you start.

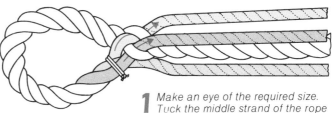

**1** Make an eye of the required size. Tuck the middle strand of the rope end under one strand of the standing part, against the lay. Tuck the second strand of the end part over the next strand of the standing part of the rope and pull tight.

**2** Turn the splice over and tuck the last full strand under the remaining strand in the rope. Pull tight again.

**3** Continue tucking each strand in turn alternatively passing over and under the strands in the standing part. Pull tight after each series of tucks.

**4** When you have completed five tucks in each strand, cut off the loose ends. You can taper the strands for the last two tucks to give a neater appearance.

# Handling ropes

The running rigging of the boat is usually made of rope (although parts of the halyards may be of wire), and since sails have to be hoisted and lowered rapidly, and mooring lines rigged quickly, you must be able to handle rope correctly. The types of rope and the different knots that can be used have already been explained. However, you also need to know how to coil rope so that it doesn't twist and become difficult to unravel. Any surplus rope should always be coiled up neatly, never left lying in a tangle where it could trip someone up. You may also occasionally have to throw a line to the shore or to another boat (known as heaving a line). If you do not do this correctly, the rope will tangle and fall short of the objective.

*Some of the many types of rope available. The most popular varieties are described on page 146.*

# Cleating a rope

It is essential to cleat a rope correctly or it may slip or even jam immovably. The cleat, of course, must be large enough to take the rope, and with no sharp edges on which it could chafe. Lead the rope first to the part of the cleat furthest away from it. Then take one full turn around the base of the cleat, before making a figure of eight turn by winding the rope over one horn of the cleat and diagonally across the cleat before making another turn on the opposite horn. You can then finish off with a final full turn around the cleat, or you can make a locking turn (below), except when cleating sheets and halyards.

*Left, with synthetic mooring rope, you may find it better to add a locking turn to the final figure of eight. Simply slip a loop through an additional turn on the cleat.*

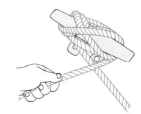

**1** *Lead the rope to the back of the cleat and take a turn around the base.*

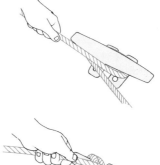

**2** *Make several figure of eight turns around the cleat.*

**3** *Finish off with a full turn around the base of the cleat.*

# Coiling a rope

Always coil any spare line neatly and secure it. There are several methods for securing a coil of rope. If you are coiling and stowing a spare line, make the coils as shown in step 1, right, leaving about 2m (6ft) of the end free. Wrap the end of the rope several times around the middle of the coil, loop the end and pass it through the coil, and drop it over the top. If you are securing the rope on a cleat, use the method shown below.

**1** Hold the rope in one hand close to the cleat and coil the surplus in a clockwise direction, making a clockwise twist as you form each loop, so that the coil lies flat.

**2** Continue forming loops until all the rope is neatly coiled.

**3** Pass your hand through the coil and grasp the part leading from the cleat.

**4** Pull this part back through the coil and twist it two or three times.

**5** Hang the loop on the top horn of the cleat The coil will then hang neatly down from it.

# Heaving a line

You may often need to heave a line to someone on another boat or on a quayside. Always coil the rope anew — don't rely on a previously coiled rope which may be twisted or kinked. You should also check first that the line is long enough to reach the objective before throwing it. Coil the rope clockwise in the usual way, making a clockwise twist in each loop so that the coils lie flat. If you are right-handed, stand with your left shoulder towards your objective, divide the coil evenly into two parts and hold one in each hand. Then throw the rope in your right hand, swinging your arm back in an underarm motion, and aiming slightly higher than the objective. Release the remaining coils, but hold onto the end!

**1** Divide the correctly formed coils into two parts, holding one in each hand.

**2** Swing your throwing arm back in an underarm arc, and aim slightly higher than your objective.

**3** Release the coil in your throwing hand, and let the remainder of the coil in your other hand run free.

# GLOSSARY

## A

**Aback** Said of a sail when, with its clew to windward, it is pressed back against the mast.

**Abaft** At right angles to the centreline of the boat.

**Adrift** A free, floating object which is unable to move under its own power.

**Aft** Towards, near or at the stern. It may also be behind the stern.

**Afterpart** The part of the boat behind the beam.

**A-hull** A boat is a-hull when it is hove-to with all its sails furled.

**Aloft** Overhead.

**Amidships** The middle of the boat, either fore, aft or athwartships.

**Anchorage** The ground in which an anchor is laid; it usually denotes a sheltered area with good holdiing ground and the lack of strong tides.

**Anti-fouling** A paint compound used to protect the underwater part of a boat from the growth of marine life.

**Apparent wind** The wind that flows from a moving boat – the sum of the true and the created wind.

**Astern** Behind the boat.

**Athwartship** At right angles to the fore-and-aft line of a vessel.

## B

**Back a sail** To push a sail out so that the wind fills it from the opposite side.

**Bail** To remove water from an open boat.

**Ballast** Weight, usually metal, placed low on the boat, or externally on the keel, to provide stability.

**Bare poles, to sail under** To sail without any sails set.

**Batten** A light wooden or plastic strip inserted into a pocket in a sail to support the roach.

**Beam** The width of the boat at its widest point.

**Bear away** To alter course away from the wind.

**Bear down** To approach something from upwind.

**Beating** To sail to windward close-hauled, on a zig-zag course, to reach an objective to windward.

## B

**Becket** A loop or a small eye in the end of a rope or a block.

**Bend** (1) To attach a sail to its spar; (2) to attach two ropes together by means of a knot.

**Bermudan rig** A rig in which the mainsail is triangular.

**Bight** A loop in a rope.

**Block** The nautical term for a pulley.

**Boeier** Small 17th-century Dutch yacht.

**Bolt rope** A reinforcing rope along the edge of a sail.

**Boom** A spar which is used to extend the foot of a sail.

**Bottlescrew** A metal screw fitting used for adjusting tension on shrouds and stays at the lower (deck) end.

**Bow** The forward part of a vessel.

**Bowsprit** A spar which projects from the bow of a boat, used to extend the sail area.

**Broach** The action of a boat when running before a sea, it slews round inadvertently, broadside-on to the waves.

**Burgee** Small triangular flag flown from the top of the mast. It indicates the direction of the apparent wind.

**By-the-lee** Sailing on a run, but with the wind blowing from the leeward side of the boat.

## C

**Cable** The rope or chain attached to an anchor.

**Camber** (1) The curve of the deck from one side of the boat to the other; (2) the curve of a sail.

**Carvel** Form of wooden boat construction in which timber planks are laid flush over wooden ribs.

**Caulking** Fibre and compound placed between planking to make it watertight.

**Centreboard** A pivoting plate of wood used to lessen leeway.

**Centreline** The centre of the boat, on a fore-and-aft line.

**Chainplates** Metal fittings on the side of a boat to which the shrouds are attached.

**Chine** The angle of a junction between two flat sides of a hull.

## C

**Chord** An imaginary line between the luff and the leech of a sail, parallel to the foot.

**Chute** An opening in the deck, near the bow, from which the spinnaker is hoisted.

**Claw ring** A C-shaped fitting which can be slipped over the boom – for example when the sail has been roller reefed, to allow the kicking strap to be re-attached.

**Cleat** A wooden or metal fastening around which ropes can be made fast.

**Clew** The lower after corner of a fore-and-aft sail.

**Clinker** A form of wooden hull construction in which planks are laid fore-and-aft, overlapping at the edges.

**Close-hauled** Said of a boat which, with its sheets pulled in, is sailing as close to the wind as possible.

**Compass** An instrument used to indicate direction relative to the earth's magnetic field.

**Cringle** A loop or eye set into the bolt rope of a sail.

**Cross-trees** Metal or wooden struts attached to the mast on either side to increase the spread, and thus the holding power, of the main shrouds.

**Crutch** (see *Rowlock*)

**Cunningham hole** An eye in the luff of a sail above the tack which allows the tension of the luff to be adjusted.

**Cutter** A single masted fore-and-aft sailing boat with an inner staysail and outer jib. It can be gaff-rigged or Bermudan-rigged.

## D

**Daggerboard** A board in the centre of a boat, which can be raised or lowered, and is used to prevent sideslip.

**Deck** Covering of the interior of a boat, either carried completely over it or over a portion of it.

**Displacement** The weight of water displaced by a floating boat (the weight is the same as that of the boat itself).

**Double-ender** A boat with a pointed bow and stern.

**Downhaul** Tackle used to pull down the tack and thus tension the luff of a sail.

**Draught** Vertical distance

measured from the waterline to the lowest point of the hull.

**Draw** A sail is said to be drawing when it is filled.

**Drogue** Object towed over boat's stern in order to reduce speed.

## E

**Ease** To let out a sheet or line gradually.

**Ebb** A falling tide (going out).

**Ensign** A nautical version of the national flag of a boat's country of registration. It is flown at the stern.

## F

**Fairlead** Any ring, bolt, eye or loop used to guide a rope in the required direction.

**Fairway** Main channel down which boats should proceed in restricted waters.

**Fall** The part of a rope which is hauled on in a tackle.

**Fathom** A measurement of water depth: one fathom equals six feet.

**Fender** A cushion of durable material inserted between a boat and some other object in order to prevent contact or chafe.

**Fetch** To sail close-hauled without having to tack.

**Fin keel** Single, ballasted keel attached centrally to the bottom of the hull.

**Flood** A rising tide (coming in).

**Flotsam** Any of the contents or equipment of a boat which have been washed overboard.

**Fluke** The points of an anchor.

**Following sea** A sea which is travelling in the same direction as the boat.

**Foot** The lower edge of a sail.

**Fore** Towards, near or at the bow.

**Fore-and-aft** In line from bow to stern; on, or parallel to, the centreline.

**Forepeak** A space in the bows of a vessel, right forward.

**Foresail** Triangular-shaped sail set before the mast.

**Forestay** A stay leading from the masthead to the bow, to stop the mast falling backwards.

**Foul** To entangle or obstruct.

**Freeboard** The portion of a vessel's hull which is not submerged.

**Freer** A wind shift further aft relative to the boat.

**Furl** To roll a sail and secure it to its yard or boom.

## G

**Gaff** A spar which extends the head of a four-sided, fore-and-aft mainsail.

**Go about** To turn the bows of the boat through the wind, so as to put it on the opposite tack.

**Gooseneck** The universal joint fitting on a mast to which the boom is attached.

**Goosewing** To sail before the wind with the mainsail set on one side of the boat and the jib set on the other.

**Grommet** A ring of rope, or a loop formed at the end of a rope.

**Ground tackle** Generic term for anchoring equipment.

**GRP** Glass reinforced plastic: a material used for boat construction, it comprises fibreglass cloth impregnated with polyester resins.

**Gudgeon** Fitting on the stern of a boat into which the pintle of the rudder is inserted, enabling the rudder to pivot.

**Gunter rig** A rig whereby a gaff slides up a mast to form an extension to the mast.

**Gunwale** The upper edge of the side of the hull.

**Gybe** The swinging over of a fore-and-aft sail when running before the wind. It may be a controlled manoeuvre when a boat is changing its course, or it can happen accidentally.

## H

**Halyard** A rope, wire or chain by which a sail, flag or yard is hoisted.

**Hanks** Rings or catch-hooks by which sails are attached to stays.

**Hard eye** A reinforced wire loop.

**Harden up** To sail a boat closer to the wind.

**Header** A wind shift further aft relative to the boat.

**Heading** The direction in which a boat is pointing.

**Headsail** A sail set forward of the main mast.

**Head-to-wind** With the bow facing into the wind.

**Heave-to** (1) To stop the boat by backing the jib and lashing the tiller; (2) to slow the boat by letting the sails flap on a beam reach (used for short periods only).

**Heel** (1) A boat is said to heel when it lies over at an angle when sailing; (2) the bottom end of the mast.

**Helm** The steering apparatus.

**Helmsman** One who steers.

**Holding ground** The part of the sea bed where the anchor digs in.

**Hove-to** (see *Heave-to*).

**Hull speed** The maximum speed a hull not capable of planing can achieve.

## I

**In irons** A boat is said to be in irons when it has stopped head-to-wind, or is moving backwards.

**IYRU** International Yacht Racing Union. A body which controls and administers international yacht racing.

## J

**Jackyard** A yard or pole extending the head or foot of the topsail beyond the topmast of the gaff of a gaff-rigged boat.

**Jamming cleat** A cleat designed to allow a rope to be made fast quickly by jamming it.

**Jetsam** Anything thrown overboard.

**Jib** The foremost sail; it is a fore-and-aft' triangular sail.

**Jury rig** A temporary replacement of any part of the boat's rigging, set up after damage or breakage, which enables the boat to be sailed.

## K

**Kedge** (1) A small auxiliary anchor; (2) to kedge is to move a vessel by laying out the kedge and pulling on it.

**Keel** The fixed underwater part of a sailing boat used to prevent sideways drift and provide stability.

**Ketch** A two-masted, fore-and-aft rigged boat. The forward mast is the mainmast – the mizzen mast, stepped aft, is always forward of the rudder post.

**Kicking strap** Line which stops the boom from rising when the mainsail is set.

**King post** A vertical post, usually employed as a support.

**Knot** A nautical mile covered in one hour.

## L

**Lacing** A length of line or thin rope.

**Landfall** Arrival at land.

**Lanyard** A short line or rope used to attach one object to another.

**Lashing** A rope used for securing any movable object.

**Lay up** To store a yacht during the winter.

**Lazy guy** A guy (or rope) which is not in use and is taking no strain.

**Lazyjacks** Ropes extending from the boom to the mast, to help gather in a sail when lowering it.

**Lead** (1) A lead weight which is attached to the end of a line and used to ascertain the depth of water beneath a boat and the nature of the bottom. The weight and line together is known as the hand-lead; (2) the path taken by a rope, usually between a sail and a fairlead or winch.

**Lee** (1) Area away from the wind (downwind); (2) to be in the lee of an object is to be sheltered by it.

**Leeboards** Boards fixed vertically to the outside of the hull to prevent leeway.

**Leech** The aftermost edge of a fore-and-aft sail; both side edges of a square sail.

**Leeward** The distance between the course steered by a vessel and that actually run.

**Let fly** To let a sheet go, thus spilling the wind from a sail.

**Lie** To remain without motion – more precisely, it means to keep a boat as steady as possible in a gale.

**Lifeline** Safety line fitted around an open deck of a yacht.

**Loose** (1) To loose a rope is to let it go; (2) to loose a sail

is to unfurl or set it.

**Loose-footed** A sail not laced by its foot to a boom.

**Low water** The lowest level reached by each tide.

**Luff** (1) The forward edge of a sail; (2) to luff is to bring the vessel's head closer to the wind; (3) to luff up or luff round is to turn the vessel head-to-wind.

**Lug (or lugsail)** A four-sided sail, bent onto a yard, and slung to the mast in a fore-and-aft position. There are three kinds: a standing or working lug, a dipping lug and a balanced lug.

**Lugger** A boat, usually for fishing, rigged with lugsails.

## M

**Make fast** To secure a rope.

**Marconi** An alternative name for a Bermudan rig.

**Mark** An object used as a guide while navigating.

**Marline spike** A pointed tapering iron or wooden spike used for opening the strands of rope when splicing.

**Mast** A pole, or system of attached poles, placed vertically on a vessel, used to spread the sails.

**Mast gate** The point at which the mast passes through the foredeck of a dinghy.

**Masthead** The top of a mast.

**Masthead sloop** A sloop where the forestay, on which the foresail is set, reaches to the masthead.

**Mast step** A recess in a vessel's keel into which the base of the mast is positioned.

**Metre class** A form of rating for a boat based on a certain measurement formula.

**Miss stays** A sailing vessel is said to miss stays when it fails to go about while tacking.

**Mizzen** (1) The aftermost mast of various rigs; (2) a fore-and-aft sail hoisted on the mizzen mast.

**Moor** To fasten a vessel to a mooring.

**Mooring** Any arrangement of anchors and cables which are permanently laid.

**Moulded hull** One which is built up by bonding layers of veneer or of GRP.

# N

**Nautical almanac** An annual book containing astronomical and tidal information for the use of sailors and navigators.
**Nautical mile** One 60th of a degree of latitude (a minute); slightly longer than a standard mile.
**No go zone** Area into which a boat cannot sail without tacking.

# O

**Offshore** Away from the shore.
**Offwind** Any point of sailing away from the wind.
**One-design** Any boat built to conform to rules so that it is identical to all others in the same class.
**Onshore** Towards the shore.
**Outhaul** A rope which hauls out something, as the clew outhaul does the clew of the mainsail.
**Outpoint** To sail closer to the wind than another boat.

# P

**Paddle** A small oar; it is used to propel a boat over the side or stern.
**Painter** A rope attached to the bow of a small boat, by which it may be made fast.
**Peak** (1) The upper corner of a four-sided sail, usually applied to a gaff sail; (2) the upper end of a gaff.
**Pennant** A long triangular flag.
**Pilot** (1) A person licensed to navigate vessels through channels, and in and out of port; (2) Admiralty sailing directions.
**Pinch** To sail too close to the wind.
**Pintle** Metal pin on boat's stern post on which the rudder hangs by its gudgeons.
**Pitch** (1) The residuum of boiled tar used for caulking; (2) the downward motion of the bows of a boat plunging into the trough of a wave.
**Pitch-pole** Said of a boat which somersaults stern-over-bow, usually after being up-ended by a wave.
**Plane** To gain hydro-dynamic lift as the boat lifts up on its bow wave.

**Planking** The covering of the ribs of a hull with wooden planks.
**Plot** To mark courses, bearings and directions on a chart.
**Point high** To sail very close to the wind.
**Points of sailing** The different courses on which a boat may sail.
**Pontoon** A low, flat, floating platform, normally used as a launching site at the water's edge.
**Port** The left-hand side of a vessel when looking forwards. A boat is on "port tack" when the wind is blowing over its port side.
**Preventer** Additional stay line or tackle set up to prevent movement in a mast or boom. A boom preventer is a line or tackle set up to prevent an accidental gybe.
**Protest flag** Flag hoisted during a race when a boat is fouled by another competitor.
**Prow** The bows and fore part of a vessel.
**Punt** Flat-bottomed boat, square at each end, and usually propelled by a pole. Only suitable for shallow inland waterways.
**Purchase** Any tackle or manner of leverage used to raise or move some object.

# Q

**Quarter** The portion of the ship midway between the beam and the stern. "On the quarter" applies to a bearing 45° abaft the beam.
**Quartering** With the wind or waves on the quarter.

# R

**Race** A strong tide or current.
**Range** (1) The length of rope or chain required for any particular purpose. The range of the cable is the length of chain drawn out on deck prior to anchoring; (2) the difference in the depth of the water between high and low tides.
**Rating** A method of measuring certain dimensions of yachts of different sizes and types so that they can race on a handicap basis.
**Reach** (1) To sail with the

wind approximately abeam; (2) the distance between two bends of a river.
**"Ready about"** An order to stand by when tacking, in preparation for going about onto the opposite tack.
**Reef** To reduce the sail area by folding or rolling.
**Reef bands** Horizontal strengthening bands of canvas running across a sail, perforated with holes or eyes, used to hold reef points.
**Reef cringles** The eyes or loops on the leech of the sail through which the reef lines are passed, and used for securing the cringle of a reefed sail to the boom.
**Reef points** Short pieces of rope hung on each side of the sail, from the eyes in the reef band, used for tying up the reefed portion of the sail.
**Reeve** To pass something through a hole. To "reeve a tackle" is to pass a rope through the blocks.
**Restricted class** A class of boats all of a particular set or fixed dimensions but with others which may vary.
**Ribs** The timbers which form the frame or skeleton of a boat, to which the planking is secured.
**Ride** (1) To lie at anchor; (2) to ride out a gale is to wait for a gale to pass when at sea.
**Rig** The form or manner in which a vessel's mast, spars and sails are arranged.
**Rigging** The wires and ropes employed to keep the mast in place and to work the sails. (See *Running rigging* and *Standing rigging*).
**Rise** The rise of a tide is the height difference between low water and the sea surface at any time.
**Roach** The curved leech of a sail.
**Roadstead** An anchorage some distance from the shore.
**Rowlock** A curved metal support space in which the oar is held in place.
**Rubbing strake** Wooden beading running around the outside of a boat just beneath the gunwale to protect it against damage when touching quays, piers or other boats.
**Rudder** Movable underwater part of a vessel used for

steering, and preventing sideslip.
**Rudder post** The aftermost timber of a boat.
**Run** To sail with the wind aft.
**Running rigging** The generic term for sheets and halyards: the ropes which hoist and sheet sails.

# S

**Schooner** A boat with two or more masts, with the main-mast as the aftermost one.
**Scope** Length of rope which is paid out when anchoring the boat.
**Scull** To propel a dinghy forwards using an oar over the stern in a figure of eight movement.
**Sea breeze** An onshore breeze caused by warm air rising off the land.
**Set** (1) To set sail is to haul up the sails preparatory to starting; (2) the set of the tide is the direction of a tidal current.
**Set flying** A sail set with no stay, gaff or yard.
**Shackle key** A metal "key" for unscrewing shackle pins.
**Shake out** To cast off or loosen.
**Shank** The main shaft or leg of an anchor. A "shank painter" is a rope which holds the anchor to the vessel's deck.
**Sheave** The pulley wheel in a block and sometimes in a spar.
**Sheer** The straight or curved deck line of a vessel when viewed from the side.
**Sheet** The rope attached to the clew of a sail, used to trim it. When the sheets are brought in and made fast they are said to be sheeted home.
**Shell** The metal casing of a block; it holds the pin.
**Shock cord** A form of strong elasticated rope.
**Shrouds** Wire ropes which support the mast on either side; also referred to as the standing rigging.
**Single up** To cast off all warps except one at each position.
**Skeg** Projecting part of the underwater surface of a boat on which the rudder is hung.
**Slack tide** A short period at the turn of the tide when there is no tidal flow in

either direction.

**Slip** (1) To let go, purposely – as "to slip the anchor"; (2) A slip line is a doubled line with both ends made fast on board, so that it can be released from onboard.

**Sloop** A single-masted boat with only one headsail; it can be gaff- or Bermudan-rigged.

**Snatch block** A block into which a rope can be placed from the side without it having to be threaded through.

**Spar** A generic term for masts booms, gaffs or bowsprits.

**Spill** To spill wind is to allow a sail to shake, thus spilling the wind out of it.

**Spinnaker** A lightweight, three-cornered sail, set flying from the masthead and controlled by sheets from each clew.

**Spit** A small projection of land, or a sand bank projecting into the water at low tide.

**Splicing** A way of joining ropes by unlaying the strands and interweaving them – there are different methods for different purposes.

**Spreaders** (See *Cross-trees*)

**Sprit** A spar that extends the tack of a four-cornered sail to the peak.

**Square rig** Method of setting sails so that they hang athwart the ship. Hung on yards, the sails are four-sided.

**Stanchion** An upright post used to support the guardrails and lifelines.

**Standing rigging** The shrouds and stays which support the mast.

**Starboard** The right-hand side of the vessel looking forward. A boat is on "starboard tack" when the wind is blowing over the starboard side.

**Stays** The parts of the standing rigging which support the mast in a fore-and-aft direction.

**Staysail** A triangular head-sail hanked to a forestay.

**Steerage way** Sufficient movement through the water to enable a boat to be steered.

**Step** A recess into which the heel of the mast is placed. It

is either a wooden block or a metal frame.

**Stern** The afterpart of a vessel.

**Sternpost** The foremost timber of a vessel.

**Stock** The upper part of a rudder to which the tiller is attached.

**Sweat** To haul up tight.

# T

**Tack** (1) The forward lower corner of a fore-and-aft sail; (2) to turn the bows of a boat through the wind so that it then blows across the opposite side. A boat is said to be on port or starboard tack.

**Tackle** A purchase system of ropes and blocks, used to gain a mechanical advantage.

**Tang** A metal fitting by which stays are attached to the mast.

**Tell-tales** Small lengths of wool sewn through a sail near the luff and leech, to allow the airflow over the sail to be checked.

**Tender** A small boat used to ferry people and stores to a larger vessel.

**Thimble** A metal loop around which a rope is applied or seized to form a hard eye.

**Thwart** A seat running across a dinghy.

**Tidal atlas** Table and charts which predict the direction (or set) and speed (or drift) of tidal currents.

**Tidal stream** The horizontal movement of water caused by variations in tide height.

**Tide** Vertical rise and fall of water caused by gravitational attraction, principally of the moon.

**Tide-rode** A boat is sail to be tide-rode when it is facing into the tidal-stream, for example when moored to a buoy or anchored.

**Tideway** An area of tidal stream movement.

**Tiller** An attachment to the rudder of wood or metal, by which the rudder is controlled.

**Toestraps** Foot-loops fastened to the well of the boat, used to allow the crew to sit out and exact maximum righting leverage.

**Track** Prospective course to

be followed by the boat.

**Transit** Two objects are said to be in transit when they are in line with each other. Transits are often used as leading marks to help navigation into a harbour.

**Transom** The afterpart of the boat square to the centreline.

**Trapeze** A support used by the crew of a racing dinghy to enable him to move his weight further outboard.

**Traveller** A sliding fitting which travels on a track, used to alter sheet angles.

**True wind** The speed and direction of the wind felt by a stationary object.

# U

**Uphaul** A line used to raise any object.

# V

**Vang** A rope used to prevent a gaff or spirit from sagging to leeward.

# W

**Wake course** That actually travelled by the boat.

**Warp** Rope used to secure or move a vessel. "To warp" is to move a vessel by ropes (warps).

**Weigh anchor** To raise the anchor from the seabed.

**Whipping** Method of binding the ends of a rope to prevent them fraying.

**Whisker pole** A pole used to boom out a goosewinged jib.

**Wind-rode** Said of a boat when it faces into the wind at a mooring or anchorage.

**Windward** Towards the wind.

# Y

**Yard** A spar suspended to a mast to extend the sail area.

**Yawl** Two masted fore-and-aft rigged vessel, with the mizzen mast stepped just behind the rudder post.

# INDEX

# ACKNOWLEDGEMENTS

Photographic sources
(B = Bottom, C = Centre, T = Top, L = Left, R = Right)

Alastair Black: Half title, Title, Foreword, 10, 11, 14, 22, 23, 24, 77TL, 93, 112, 113, 116T, 122, 124R, 125, 127, 128, 130, 131, 132, 134, 135, 136, 138, 140
J. Blackman: 74
Patrick Blake: 66T, 77B
Bob Bond: 20, 73BL, 73BR, 100
Rod Carr: 88
Jack Coote: 17L
Dick Everitt: 16TR
Bob Gordon: 28, 31, 73T, 85, 89, 90, 91, 92, 114B, 115, 152
Colin Jarman: 12, 16BR, 17BR, 18L, 19, 98, 119, 120, 121, 129
Sue Rawkins: 79
Stephen Sleight: 46TC, 46TR, 123, 142, 144, 145
M. A. Stock: 16L
John Watney: 13, 15, 17TR, 18R, 75, 77TR, 81, 96, 107
Steven Wooster: 25, 27, 29, 32, 40, 42, 43, 44, 45, 46BL, 46BR, 47, 48, 49, 54, 55, 58, 59, 60, 63, 64, 65, 66BL, 66BR, 67, 68, 69, 70, 86, 95, 102, 103, 108, 114T, 116B, 117, 124L, 141

Dorling Kindersley would like to thank the following individuals and organizations for their cooperation in the production of this book.

Nigel Vick, of the Oxford and Districts Schools' Sailing Association, the staff of the National Sailing Centre, Cowes, and Julian Mannering for being prepared to sail a variety of boats in all weathers.

Steven Wooster for taking so many of the photographs and for the origination of the design, and Gillian Della Casa for her help with the design.

Capt. O. M. Watts Ltd for permission to take photographs of their chandlery.

**Illustrations by**
David Ashby
David Etchell
Andrew Farmer
John Ridyard
Les Smith
Venner Artists

**Typesetting by**
MS Filmsetting Ltd, Frome

**Reproduction by**
Reprocolor Llovet, S.A.,
Barcelona